Imperialism

Imperialism

GEORGE LICHTHEIM

PRAEGER PUBLISHERS
New York • Washington

BOOKS THAT MATTER

Published in the United States of America in 1971
by Praeger Publishers, Inc.
111 Fourth Avenue, New York, N.Y. 10003

© 1971 by Praeger Publishers, Inc.

This is a revised and expanded version of the
essays "Imperialism" and "Imperialism in This
Century," which appeared in the April and May,
1970, issues of *Commentary*, © 1970 by the American Jewish Committee.   MAY 8 7
Library of Congress Catalog Card Number: 70–117474

Printed in the United States of America

For L.H.

Contents

Imperialism

CHAPTER 1

Introduction

THE ESSAY PRESENTED HERE IS INTENDED NOT AS AN intellectual exercise but as a contribution to an ongoing political discussion. It starts, however, from the definition of a term and must therefore begin by trying to clarify what we mean when we talk about the phenomenon known as imperialism.

Theorists employ concepts as a kind of intellectual shorthand, though this is not always apparent to their readers. They use words to designate more or less complex intellectual models which have no precise equivalent in empirical reality. In this sense all theorizing is necessarily abstract and needs to be undertaken with some care, lest the unwary be misled into believing that the model employed in discourse can be encountered in the flesh outside the library or the classroom. This is never the case, for reasons which must be apparent to anyone who has thought seriously about the matter. There have been thinkers who held that to every concept there corresponds an entity properly designated by some name, but they never supposed that such entities walk about on two legs. It is only people unfamiliar with elementary logic who believe that an abstraction like "capitalism" or "imperialism" is a descriptive term to which there corresponds a slice of life that can be seen, or shown, or pointed out to by-

3

standers, as though it were a creature or an organism of some kind.

But while imperialism is not a visible thing—any more than is "the state," or "the nation," or "the commonwealth"—neither is it a mere word or an empty sound. It is indeed perfectly possible for writers to deal in verbal counters denoting nothing at all, and in some areas of literature the practice is so common that language itself tends to be devalued. But it so happens that the term "imperialism" describes a particular kind of reality, even though it is not the kind that can be statistically weighed and measured. What it denotes is a relationship: specifically, the relationship of a ruling or controlling power to those under its dominion. Empire is a state of affairs even when the imperial power is not formally constituted as such. In saying this one tacitly takes for granted the existence of political structures properly so described—that is, structures which confront the individual or the small community as an external force "alienated" from the ordinary daily routine of social production and reproduction; that is to say, one assumes a primary division between state and society, or between political and social life. Historically, this division arose from the dissolution of a more primitive mode of existence, when authority had not yet assumed the guise of an external power suspended above individuals in the form of kingship and the like. To the anthropologist, this replacement of a primitive consensus by something more in the nature of political rule is a matter of great importance, but the historian is obliged to take it for granted. It follows that we cannot here go into the question when and how something describable as a "state" arose from those features of tribal society—military leadership above all, closely followed by the taking of slaves compelled to labor for the benefit of the victorious tribe—which closely prefigure the subsequent evolution of more complex social organisms based on class and caste distinctions. For practical purposes, we can neglect tribal society, even though there have been primitive slave empires ruled by nomadic tribes.

What we mean when we speak of empire or imperialism is the relationship of a hegemonial state to peoples or nations under its control.

The introduction of the terms "people" and "nation" points to another difficulty. When we speak loosely we tend to identify these two concepts, but in strict political logic only a sovereign people can be called a nation. Sovereignty normally rests on armed force sufficient to repel invaders, and armed force commonly takes the form of some degree of centralized state power, but it need not always do so. The primitive Swiss peasant communities which repulsed the Habsburgs were armed and sovereign before they entered into the sort of political confederation that could legally be called a state. Inversely, sovereignty or independence may be internationally recognized even where there is no significant military power to speak of. The present-day Swiss Confederation is undoubtedly a sovereign state, although the time is long past when its armed forces were adequate to insure its freedom from invasion.

The purpose of these remarks is to make it clear that terms such as "empire," "state," "nation," or "sovereignty" are descriptive of something real, although there are no simple entities to which they refer. Whether or not a state is sovereign depends on its relation to other states, and the term "state" itself is applicable only under given historical conditions. There are people who lack statehood, states not founded on nationality, nation-states which either do not possess or have lost their independence, and empires not described as such in their official proclamations. In general, what people think they are doing matters considerably less than what they are in fact doing, but thought enters into the matter inasmuch as it makes possible or impossible the kind of consensus which is the foundation of every durable political arrangement. People who think of themselves not as forming a nation but rather as a congeries of tribes do not become a nation by having legal independence and a flag bestowed on them by a former colonial power, or by the United Nations. In this sense, the existence of a nation presupposes that intangible something known as "national consciousness." But the reverse is likewise true: national awareness commonly grows out of an armed struggle against hostile neighbors, or it may be started off by a revolt against foreign occupiers. Such a revolt may fail. The records of history are littered with examples of unsuccessful attempts to achieve independence, gain sovereignty, or develop a sense of nationhood. This interplay between social being and consciousness affects the consideration of our topic, for an empire is not complete without an imperial creed held by its governing class and a corresponding sense of dependence on the part of its subjects. The development of the imperial mystique commonly occurs after the event, and its ultimate perfection may actually coincide with the empire's decline from its pinnacle of power and glory; but at some stage the tacit assumptions of the ruling stratum must be made explicit. Were it otherwise, the empire would have no compass by which to steer. What the Romans thought of their *imperium* was not irrelevant. It was, among other things, an unconscious means of cementing the structure they had built.

Theories differ from poetic fabrications in that they set out to give a rational and logically consistent account of some aspect of reality. But whatever may be the case in the natural sciences, no political theory is ever purely descriptive. It always includes norms and valuations as well as factual analysis. In this respect a theory of imperialism cannot escape the rule governing social and political theorizing generally. However closely it sticks to the facts—or rather to the available empirical evidence about them—it carries a built-in reference to the general philosophy of the theorist. If he adheres to the tenets of Enlightenment rationalism and to the kind of democratic faith commonly associated with the American and French Revolutions, his view of the topic will be colored by assumptions which are by no means universally shared. He will, for example, take it for granted that there is something unnatural or immoral about the mere

existence of an empire, since it implies subordination to a
hegemonial power, whereas in principle all nations ought to be
free and equal, their internal affairs at least not being subject to
the veto power of an imperial government. The very term "imperialism" nowadays carries unflattering connotations, but it did
not do so for the ruling classes of the Roman Empire, or for the
rulers of the nominally Christian kingdoms which succeeded it.
During the lengthy epoch of the European Middle Ages, the
term "Holy Roman Empire" was applied inconsistently—and
sometimes absurdly—but always in a laudatory sense to a large
and ramshackle political structure which in practice enabled
the German Emperor, with the connivance of the Pope, to lord
it over German vassals and Italian city-states. The empires of
the Ottoman Turks, the Habsburgs, and the Romanovs all
gloried in their real or fancied magnificence, and so at a later
date did the British Empire. A *theory* of how these political
structures came into being need not, and normally does not,
reflect the values incorporated in the *ideologies* which helped
to keep them going. But in subjecting these ideologies to critical
analysis, the historian commits himself to a different set of valuations.

This is true even if the theory affirms no more than the inevitability of some sort of power balance between rival empires,
for to do so is to ascribe a rational purpose to what in other
circumstances might appear irrational—notably the act of going
to war. *A fortiori,* if the historian asserts, for example, that for
its time the Habsburg Empire performed a useful service in
keeping the Turks out of Central Europe, he is clearly committed
to a value judgment. This is also the case if he affirms the opposite, or if he judges that, as between the Turks and the
Habsburgs, there was little to choose. Again, a historian who
retrospectively welcomes the despotic unification of India or
China, on the grounds that centralization was preferable to constant warfare, is clearly making an evaluative assertion. But
suppose he merely describes the process as inevitable? It will then

be necessary to inquire into his grounds for holding such a belief, and normally it will turn out that he is able to back his conviction by theoretical arguments only because he already carries in his mind a notion of historical inevitability according to which the unification of a large territory by its rulers is both necessary and "progressive": that is, beneficial to mankind in general and the inhabitants of one particular area in particular. But what if the writer is an anarchist who on principle dislikes the establishment of states, small or great, although he may concede that it cannot be prevented? In that case, the "progressive" aspect of the phenomenon will not be apparent to him, and the argument will be deprived of its prescriptive nature. It will resume itself into a bare recitation of what actually took place.

To grasp what is at stake in political debates having to do with the conflicting claims of nationalism and imperialism, one must be clear as to the difference between sovereignty and authority. All sorts of public bodies, from churches and political parties to trade unions and professional organizations, lay claim to some degree of authority, whether legal or moral. But authority is one thing, sovereignty is another. A state is sovereign to the extent that it possesses a political center whose decisions override the will of all subordinate authorities; it is sovereign in respect of the outside world to the degree to which it can enforce its legal authority. If it is invaded by armed force and fails to resist, its authority vanishes together with its sovereignty, and this is the case whatever its social structure, legal fabric, constitutional façade, or political regime. It is pointless to inquire whether it is "in the nature" of this or that form of social organization—feudalism, capitalism, socialism, or whatever—to encourage or permit external aggression against weaker states. The only thing that matters to those concerned is the actual possession or loss of their freedom. If a country is invaded by a stronger power and its political institutions are destroyed or remolded, that country is under imperial domination, whatever the political circumstances of the case, and whether or not the whole transaction is classifiable as "progressive" or "reactionary," according to some canon of historical interpretation. Likewise, sovereignty may be infringed by diplomatic means, by treaty, or by economic pressure. A backward country legally prevented from developing its industries suffers a loss of sovereignty no less real because it may be invisible to the naked eye of the beholder. What counts is the relationship of domination and subjection, which is the essence of every imperial regime.

The word "essence" conjures up the dismaying prospect of a scholastic debate as to the existence or nonexistence of entities not observable in ordinary experience. But we are not obliged to involve ourselves in such a disputation. To say that it is "of the essence" of imperialism to infringe the sovereignty of lesser political bodies is not to engage in metaphysics, but to define the proper use of a term commonly employed by everyone who thinks about public affairs. We do not thereby commit ourselves to the notion that there is a disembodied entity called "imperialism" which moves mysteriously behind the scenes of history. We simply specify the minimum criteria for the use of language when dealing with a particular reality familiar to millions of ordinary people who have the misfortune to be involved in imperialist rivalries. At the same time we avoid the intellectual dishonesty which marks the propagandistic employment of the term by one side or the other in what is vulgarly known as the cold war (itself a propaganda term invented to describe the Soviet-American rivalry consequent upon the Yalta and Potsdam settlements of 1945). We specify criteria for the use of language which cannot be misused because they cut across the quarrel between the nuclear superpowers. Propagandists use words like flags. In what follows we shall abstain from this familiar custom. Instead we shall concentrate upon the actual relationships that give rise to the spectacle of hegemonial power. For a start, let us inquire into the genesis of the term "empire."

It will then become apparent that in so doing we are laying bare at least some of the historical roots of the phenomenon known as imperialism.

This topic inevitably entails a reconsideration of both the liberal and the socialist heritage, inasmuch as both schools attempted, from about 1900, to grapple with the theory and practice of modern imperialism. The inadequacy of liberal thinking in this field is now pretty generally recognized, not least by the surviving liberals, some of whom have in consequence helped themselves to large slices of socialist theorizing in an effort to buttress their own position. With the socialist theory of imperialism one runs into a different problem. Historically, modern imperialism and modern socialism gained prominence from the 1880's onward in response to the evident decline of liberalism in general and Anglo-American liberalism in particular. Stemming as they did from opposite poles of the political compass—imperialism from the ruling class, socialism from its enemies—they reached different conclusions. But they overlapped in those spheres of public life where conservatives and socialists came to challenge the liberal consensus that had originally been established during the mid-Victorian era. Hence the peculiar phenomenon of "social imperialism," an ideology which sought to combine protectionist defense of the "national interest" with social-reformist attempts to improve the condition of the working class in the imperial metropolis. The eventual fusion of social imperialism with Social Darwinism, in the theory and practice of European fascism during the 1930's and 1940's, has discredited this experiment so far as the labor movement and the historic Left are concerned. It has done little to lessen its attraction for non-European aspirants to the imperial succession, and it has even infected the ideology of nationalist movements stemming from the Third World of underdeveloped countries.

A different sort of problem arises in connection with the Marxist tradition properly so described. Down to the Russian Revolution, this tradition found its adherents primarily in

Western and Central Europe. These writers already possessed a
theory of imperialism prior to 1917, but were unable to relate it
to the ongoing practice of the parties affiliated with the Second
International founded in 1889. The overriding fact for most
socialists during the pre-1914 age was the persistence of the
ancient dynastic structures in Central and Eastern Europe: Imperial Germany, Austria-Hungary, and Czarist Russia, to which
Ottoman Turkey might be added. In consequence, anti-imperialism came to be identified with the cause of national liberation
from archaic political constraints, whereas the specifically Marxist
analysis of capitalist imperialism attracted the attention of only
a few theorists. This situation altered radically with the Russian
Revolution, the Bolshevik triumph, and the emergence of what
is still officially known as Marxism-Leninism. As a result of
Lenin's intervention, imperialism became a major concern for
Communists, that is, for Marxists who associated themselves with
the Third International and its Trotskyist or Maoist offsprings.
The consequences of this realignment will be examined at some
length in the later chapters of this study. Here let it simply be
said that the identification of Marxism with Leninism has become untenable, not least because the Sino-Soviet conflict cannot
be explained in Leninist terms. Fifty years after Lenin, it is increasingly evident that theoretical explanations put forward
around 1920 to account for the genesis of the 1914–18 war do not
help one to make sense of the contemporary world scene. This is
no reason for casting the Marxist apparatus overboard in favor
of earlier and simpler conceptualizations, but neither does it
permit the unmediated use of notions which possessed practical
relevance half a century ago, but have now been turned into
empty slogans. Marxism is too important to be left to the post-
Leninist sects—tiny ferocious creatures devouring each other in
a drop of water.

What remains of the fragile synthesis known as Marxism-
Leninism, now that the Soviet Union has joined the ranks of the
nuclear superpowers and seems bent on playing the imperial

game at the expense of the Third World, is the general perspective of an age of revolutionary convulsions set off by imperialist conflicts. In principle this outlook is not incompatible with parallel notions emanating from the political Right. The earlier convergence of Darwinism and expansionism has found a modern successor in the technocratic vision of a planetary economy controlled by a unified elite of scientifically trained managers who have left the national state behind and merged their separate identities in the formation of a global cartel linking all the industrially advanced centers of the world: "ultra-imperialism" to employ Kautsky's phrase. This gloomy vision, first formulated in 1914 by the principal theorist of the Second International, looks remarkably modern today: more so than the productions of the rival Leninist school. Whether it is going to be validated by experience, no one can say. What should be emphasized is that we have no theoretical grounds for dismissing this hypothesis as an aberration. More generally, it needs to be said that the train called "history" is never going to deposit its passengers at the destination of their choice unless they themselves take over the controls. Faith in automatic progress ought to have died in 1914. Where it still persists, it does so as a carry-over from the genial optimism of the nineteenth century—an optimism Marx did not share. Those who consider themselves his disciples can do no better, in view of what this generation has experienced and what is still to come, than to arm themselves with the motto of those ancient warriors, the French Huguenots: *"Point n'est besoin d'espoir pour entreprendre, ni de succès pour persévérer."*

CHAPTER 2

Imperium

"CICERO'S COMMENTS ON THE *imperium populi Romani* never swerved from the intrinsic meaning of 'imperium' to which he paid emphatic tribute in *De Legibus*—the legal power to enforce the law."[1] This observation by a distinguished historian illustrates some of the difficulties of our theme. In itself, the remark just quoted is enlightening inasmuch as it bears upon the mentality of the Roman oligarchy and the characteristic features of the ideology it had built up. At the same time it is plain that we are not really being told anything about the actuality of the Empire which Cicero helped to govern while it was still a Republic, and whose control was subsequently inherited by Caesar. From the standpoint of both Caesar and Cicero, the fact that the "Empire of the Roman People" was a slave state whose economy rested upon servile labor did not enter into consideration when they sought to define the political entity known to them and their contemporaries as the *Imperium populi Romani*. Not that they were unaware of the circumstance: it simply did not occur to them that any other form of social organization was possible, let alone desirable. Similarly, they took it for granted that the Roman people—or to be exact, its governing class—ruled over subject populations which, though

13

once free, had come under the political sway of the Roman Senate. Cicero's writings are indeed full of warnings about the dangers of moral decay threatening the Republic from the uncontrolled extension of imperial dominance over other peoples, but what concerned him was the political health of the *res pub- lica*—the public body to which he belonged and of which he was such a distinguished ornament. That it was Rome's destiny to rule the lesser breeds went without saying. A generation later, in the age of Augustus, there arose a group of poets who poured the new imperial faith into the ancient bottle of rhetoric. Horace, Virgil, and Ovid sang the glories of Augustus and the Empire: Horace composed a hymn to "The Age of Caesar," Ovid described Rome as the seat of the immortal gods, and Virgil opened his epic, the *Aeneid,* with a divine prophecy assuring the refugees fleeing from the ruins of Troy that from them would descend a people destined for boundless expansion and endowed with "unending empire."

If this sounds remarkably modern, the reason is quite simply that in the West we have all been influenced by the Greek and Roman classics, so that Europe's poets inevitably fell into similar strains when they felt like celebrating the glories of whatever empire happened to be on top at the moment. In studying the historian's account of our predecessors we cannot fail to be struck by certain similarities, despite differences attributable to the rise of Christianity and the consequent abandonment of mental traits which went unchallenged in antiquity. No modern writer would be so naive as to attribute eternity—in the literal sense of the term—to the empire of which he is a citizen. On the other hand, those Roman historians and poets who worked the theme of moral earnestness have had their modern successors. "Livy, in his Preface, expresses anxieties even more sombre than those of the early Horace concerning the moral adequacy of his contemporaries to meet their imperial duties. The nations of the world still stand in awe of the Romans. They have resigned themselves to the *imperium.* But the purpose of the historian must be to show the contrast between the Romans of yore and those of the latest generations."[2] The Empire—no longer a republican *Imperium populi Romani,* but converted by the Augustans into a distinctly monarchical *Imperium Romanum*—needed conscientious governors, but in the new post-republican era such citizens were hard to find. The *imperium* had been created during the heroic age of the Republic—and then had killed its parent. It was now governed by the *Princeps* and his officials, but these men lacked the austere virtues of their forefathers: or so at least Livy thought, and his gloomy forebodings later found an echo in the writings of Seneca—not accidentally a convert to Stoicism. Tacitus too had his doubts as to the permanence of the Empire, and took no trouble to hide them. The Augustan Principate, after all, had arisen from an act of usurpation, and Tacitus knew that the constitutional façade concealed the reality of military power. If the army could make an Emperor, it could also unmake him. *"Evulgato imperii arcano posse principem alibi quam Romae fieri"*: the secret was out that an Emperor could be made elsewhere than at Rome and other than constitutionally by the Senate. And what was the imperial Senate anyway? For the most part no longer an assembly of proud and independent aristocrats, but a collection of officeholders whose tenure depended in large part on the grace and favor of the *Princeps.* Yet the great historian was himself a Roman Senator, Consul and Proconsul of Asia. More important, he formed part of the ruling oligarchy whose deeds he described in language at once stately and eloquent. "Oligarchy is the supreme, central, and enduring theme in Roman history. Across the revolutionary age it links the aristocratic Republic to the monarchy of the Caesars; and the process of change in the governing order has its sequel in the century between Caesar Augustus and Trajan."[3]

Oligarchy is the secret, too, of the *Imperium Romanum,* for the people—as distinct from the governing class—had little to do with its inception. They fought and bled in the wars that transformed the landlocked Roman Republic into an empire, but

to them these were wars against foreign invaders. It was the ruling class of great families who converted the nascent empire
into something else: a hegemonial power centered upon control
of the Mediterranean. Having created this structure, the oligarchy
gave birth to a culture which simultaneously reflected and shaped
the norms and values that went into the constitution of the
imperium. These values were in the first place military and
patriotic, but in due course they were reshaped and redefined so
as to make room for the new emotion of imperialism. The
emotive significance of the term *imperium* had originally been
derived from Rome's long struggle against foreign enemies, the
Carthaginians above all. In the course of these protracted wars,
the Roman peasantry, which bore the chief burden of conscription, was ruined economically, and in consequence weakened
politically—to such a degree that the ruling nobility became for
practical purposes all-powerful. The only constraint upon it
arose from the necessity of feeding and flattering an urban mob,
which was kept quiet with the help of plunder extorted from
the conquered provinces. The *Imperium populi Romani* thus
paid off, so far as the mob of the capital city was concerned, and
it threw open tremendous avenues of prestige and wealth for
the ruling aristocracy, both under the late Republic and after
the advent of Caesarism. The Caesars still had to feed the
Roman mob—mainly with foodstuffs collected from North Africa
—and they also had to keep the Praetorian Guard happy by
constant increases in pay. But their chief concern was the
permanent state of war on the Empire's frontiers: in Spain and
in Africa, on the Danube and in Germany, as well as in Syria
and along the border with Persia. Contrary to legend, Rome
was not seriously bothered by slave revolts. No slave rising in
antiquity was permanently successful, and none shook the power
of the governing class. The freeborn Roman mob was no longer
a major problem either, since it had been disarmed and deprived
of political power. The real threat to stability arose from the

army and from the foreign barbarians whom it was holding down.

The *imperium* was thus at once the creation and the plaything of a self-perpetuating oligarchy, and the latter—like every ruling class in history—had its great men: Scipio, victor in the long war against Hannibal which at one point threatened Rome's very existence; Julius Caesar; Cicero, orator and statesman; Livy and Tacitus among historians; Horace and Virgil among poets; Seneca, more remarkable perhaps for the dignified manner of his death under Nero than for his attempt to acclimatize Greek Stoicism in Rome; and a host of lesser figures. Together they embodied the values of their culture and created the first successful imperialist ideology in history. The special mark of this ideology was moral earnestness, allied to a strong distaste for Greek frippery and Oriental self-abasement. The Roman esteem for courage, patriotism, family piety, and a certain rustic honesty, along with contempt for slaves and tyrants, formed a solid base of real virtues, and the *imperium* was sustained by them no less than by the constant exercise of armed force. Indeed the army retained its superiority only to the extent that it embodied the traditional Roman outlook, originally the outcrop of a rural culture uncorrupted by wealth and sophistication. Even after the old rustic simplicity was gone, Rome continued to be governed by men and women who believed in the ancestral virtues and for whom the *imperium* signified moral as well as military superiority over cowardly Orientals and uncouth Germans. The reader of Livy or Tacitus can discover for himself what the Roman oligarchy thought itself to be defending. Livy and Tacitus did not create the *imperium,* but they enable us, two thousand years later, to perceive what kept it going. Just as Beethoven's music cannot be understood without taking account of the French Revolution—or for that matter the French Revolution without taking account of Beethoven's music—the greatness of Tacitus as a historian reflects the greatness of the *imperium* created by the class to which he belonged and whose virtues he extolled.

These virtues were in their origin the real or idealized traits of a landed gentry which had become the effective ruling class of a rather simply structured commonwealth of patrician nobles and rural or urban plebeians: freeborn, but hampered in the exercise of their political rights until in due course they attained formal equality. As thus constituted, the Republic had only one serious business: at first, war against hostile city-states and later against rival powers in the Mediterranean. By the time these wars were concluded, the original meaning of *imperium* had been transformed. It no longer signified the authority bestowed by the Roman people upon civilian or military magistrates, but the dominion of Rome over others. This was a development of the highest significance, for it colored the whole subsequent course of Western political history and, more especially, the coinage of Western political terminology. That a Roman commander was *cum imperio* originally meant that he had been entrusted by the Senate and the popular assembly with supreme military responsibility. By the time the Republic had acquired an empire, the term signified something quite different: that the Roman people as a whole—which by then had surrendered effective power to its governing oligarchy—was collectively entrusted with the responsibility for ruling other peoples.

The transformation was so gradual that it never occurred to anyone to question its legitimacy. Least of all did it occur to those luckless revolutionaries, the Gracchi: liberal aristocrats who appealed to the Roman people against the oligarchy and duly paid with their lives for their illusions. "Tiberius Gracchus, trying to make the Roman masses conscious of social injustice, reminded them that they were always called 'the victorious people possessed of the world.' "[4] It was the greatness of Rome that rendered the poverty of so many Roman citizens scandalous: thus ran the litany of the popular party founded by the Gracchi, continued by Marius, and ultimately inherited by Caesar—by which time the party's populist demagogy had become wholly meaningless and its mass following the willing claque of an ambitious aristocrat aiming at dictatorial power. It is not wholly useless to be reminded that Caesar won power with the aid of the *populares,* themselves the inheritors of a party founded a century earlier by the Gracchi, whose appeal to the land-hungry Roman peasantry so frightened the oligarchy that it had them murdered. The ensuing civil wars and internal convulsions, which destroyed the ancient aristocratic Republic of the *nobiles,* made the army supreme. But the army was commanded by men who had amassed fame and fortune through their rule over conquered lands. Hence the fraudulent rhetoric of the *populares*— which paved the way for Caesar and his party—invoked the theme of imperial greatness no less than did the solemn oratory of Cicero, chief apologist of the conservative aristocracy. In the end both parties, after shedding torrents of blood in a succession of civil wars lasting a century, were joined in a common ruin, and on the wreckage of the Republic there arose the new imperial structure—sociologically speaking, the creation of a unified and irremovable governing class. Aristocracy and democracy having vacated the scene, despotism took over, but it still clothed itself in republican forms. The Caesars needed an ideology to legitimize their rule, and they found it in the *imperium.* No ruling class can function without a creed. That of the new imperial oligarchy lay ready to hand, inherited from the republican past: it was only necessary to ground the effective power of the *Princeps* and his officials in the heritage of the *Imperium populi Romani,* and the Empire could be proclaimed the legitimate successor of the Republic.

The constitutional authority of the *Princeps* was in large part derived from the older magistracy of the Republic. The term *princeps* in itself did not imply monarchy; it merely stood for a particular combination of magisterial powers: governmental, judicial, military. The essential basis of the principate, the *imperium proconsulare,* was likewise derived from republican antiquity. The *imperium,* commonly described as *proconsulare,* had originally denoted the supremacy of the elected Consuls over all authorities at home or abroad. Under Augustus and his successors, it was normally coupled with the assignment of a *provincia* embracing some portion of the Empire. The formal definition of *imperium* thereafter went beyond the traditional proconsular authority in that it assigned to the *Imperator* an *imperium maius* over all governors of provinces (including those appointed by the Senate rather than by himself) and the retention of his own *imperium* in Italy even after the *Princeps* had laid down the consular powers originally bestowed by popular or senatorial election. *Princeps* and *Imperator* became one, and the holder of the title became, in point of fact, a military autocrat, although *pro forma* he was still held accountable to the Senate (the popular assembly having vanished from the scene). He no longer needed the consular power, although the office continued to exist in order to provide a career for loyal supporters drawn from the new bureaucracy. Hence, for all practical purposes, the *Princeps* became the uncontrolled governor of the state.

> He has supreme command over all troops, wheresoever stationed, with him rest all ordinances respecting their levy, payment and dismissal, the appointment of officers and regulation of the military hierarchy: senatorial proconsuls had not power over the life of a soldier; and even in their provinces he has the right to collect fiscal revenue. He levies war, makes peace or treaty, and represents the state in relation to all foreign or dependent powers. Again, he is the high admiral of the empire, with fleets near at hand; and, besides the troops attached to these, not only the praetorian guard, his proper household brigade, but even the police and night-watch of the city, owned no allegiance to any magistrate of the republic, but only to Caesar and his praefects, and formed no insignificant force at his disposal on the spot . . . and he is so far the 'imperator' of the whole Roman world, that the whole senate and people, and even the provinces, take the

'sacramentum' in his name, binding themselves in the most solemn terms to maintain his authority against all enemies, and not to hold even their own children dearer. Naturally, in time the 'imperator' and 'princeps' became synonymous.[5]

An empire has to be administered, and the administration must be military and bureaucratic: to collect taxes and defend the frontiers against hostile tribes and rival powers. It must also display a minimum of efficiency. The old oligarchic Republic was too corrupt and faction-ridden to provide the sort of bureaucratic tidiness the constantly expanding Empire required. In the end, the burden grew too heavy for the rival factions at Rome, and they were obliged to hand over power to a military dictator who in turn became a hereditary ruler. Yet the ancient forms were observed so far as possible. The victorious Caesarian party having killed the Republic, its leaders enlisted traditional verbiage to furnish themselves with a title to legitimacy. The *imperium* came in handy. It was a link with the past, and the more talk there was of it, the less did the Roman people perceive that effective power had been usurped by an uncontrollable oligarchy. Nor was it all a matter of calculation and conscious hypocrisy. Augustus doubtless knew what he was doing when he described his assumption of despotic power as the "Restoration of the Republic," but his court poets (who first put the myth of "eternal Rome" into circulation) and the great historians of the next reign may be supposed to have been sincere when they sought comfort in the notion that the *Princeps*—successor of the ancient Republican dignitaries, whose empty titles were kept up —stood at the head of something that might be termed the *Imperium populi Romani*. Men have to believe in something, and most Romans doubtless felt that being the putative rulers of an empire on which (to cite a later phrase) the sun never set was some compensation for no longer being citizens of a Republic.[6]

Yet all this does not quite explain the ease with which the *Princeps* slipped into the role of *Imperator*. The civil wars decided an issue which went back to the foundation of the Republic itself. When Cicero staked his life on the proposition that control of the highest *imperia* should be vested in the Senate and People of Rome, he was siding with the ancient oligarchy against the Caesarians, but he was also making a gesture toward the past. The republican party had in its origins been a confederation of great family clans whose power and authority antedated the foundation of the Roman State. Thereafter, for centuries, they *were* the state, and the Republic possessed meaning for them only to the extent that they were its rulers, recognized as such by the people. When these traditional assumptions collided with the claims of popular democracy and the realities of empire, a new coalition was formed by provincial military leaders and urban demagogues, the *populares*. The coalition eventually triumphed, and its leaders thereupon purged the Senate and created a new governing class. Yet in preserving the ancient republican forms—or as many of them as they could fit into the new structure—the victors paid homage to the ancestral virtues that had cemented the early Republic. These virtues rested upon family and clan loyalty, military discipline, and the defense of Rome against all comers. The *Imperium populi Romani* could be transmuted into the *Imperium orbis terrarum* only because its ruler, the *Imperator*, from time to time rendered account for his services in war and peace to his nominal sovereign, the Roman people. The ancestral traditions had been primarily military, and their preservation was a condition for the very existence of the Empire, if it was not to be overrun by foreigners. In this sense the ancient republican patriotism remained to the end the ideological sanction of what had become an empire over other people. National pride was enlisted in the service of imperialism, as it always must be. Not accidentally, the *imperium* passed from the Romans when they ceased to hold the simple faith of their rustic forefathers.

Notes

1. Richard Koebner, *Empire* (New York: Grosset & Dunlap, 1965), p. 4.

2. *Ibid.,* p. 9.

3. Ronald Syme, *Tacitus* (Oxford: Clarendon Press; New York: Oxford University Press, 1958), Preface; see also Syme, *The Roman Revolution* (Oxford: Clarendon Press; New York: Oxford University Press, 1939; 2d ed., 1952), pp. 11–12: "The political life of the Roman Republic was stamped and swayed, not by parties and programmes of a modern and parliamentary character, not by the ostensible opposition between Senate and People, *Optimates* and *Populares, nobiles* and *novi homines,* but by the strife for power, wealth and glory. The contestants were the *nobiles* among themselves, as individuals or in groups, open in the elections and in the courts of law, or masked by secret intrigue. As in its beginning, so in its last generation, the Roman Commonwealth, 'res publica populi Romani,' was a name; a feudal order of society still survived in a city-state and governed an empire. Noble families determined the history of the Republic, giving their names to its epochs."

4. Koebner, *Empire,* p. 2.

5. Henry Furneaux, ed., *The Annals of Tacitus* (Oxford: Clarendon Press, 1883; New York: Oxford University Press, 2d ed., 1896), pp. 82–83.

6. Syme, *The Roman Revolution,* pp. 313 ff. The impact of the Punic Wars on Roman society is described at great length by Arnold Toynbee, *Hannibal's Legacy: The Hannibalic War's Effects on Roman Life,* 2 vols. (London and New York: Oxford University Press, 1965), *passim.* For an analysis of the earlier Greek maritime empire and its social foundations see M. I. Finley, *The Ancient Greeks* (London: Chatto & Windus; New York: Viking Press, 1963), pp. 45 ff; A. H. M. Jones, *Athenian Democracy* (Oxford: Basil Blackwell, 1957; New York: Barnes & Noble, 1957), *passim;* T. T. B. Ryder, *Koine Eirene: General Peace and Local Independence in Ancient Greece* (London and New York: Oxford University Press, 1965); George Thomson, *Aeschylus and Athens* (London: Lawrence & Wishart, 1941; New York: Haskell House, 2d ed., 1964).

CHAPTER 3

The Rise of Europe

IF THE ROMANS INVENTED THE CONCEPT OF EMPIRE, they did not invent its reality. Dominion over other people had been the rule rather than the exception in the age of the despotic Oriental monarchies whose power antedated the Hellenic thalassocracy and its successor, the *Imperium Romanum.* The ancient Egyptian, Babylonian, and Hindu despotisms centered upon the river valleys of the Nile, the Euphrates, and the Indus. Greece and Rome extended their sway throughout the Mediterranean. Byzantium and Islam, who between them divided the Roman heritage in the East, were as imperial as their respective rulers could make them. In the West, the Catholic Church transmitted the Roman heritage to the extent of investing the barbaric Germanic kings with a spurious claim to rule over the ancient *Imperium orbis terrarum* of the Caesars. The Roman Church thus became the principal link between the *Imperium Romanum* and the Holy Roman Empire of the European Middle Ages—so called, to repeat the well-known jest, because it was neither holy, nor Roman, nor an empire. The gibe is tediously familiar. It is also misleading. The empire of Charlemagne and his Germanic successors was certainly not holy, and only doubtfully Roman (the early rulers were ignorant of Latin), but its claims were tested in warfare against rival powers and survived the exposure. This after all was what *imperium* signified. "The original Latin word conveyed the general meanings of command and power. It specifically denoted the legal power of command. Its purport was extended to include the territories and populations subject to a dominant power."[1] We have seen in the previous chapter how this process was mediated by the real or fancied interests of the ruling class which had originally created the Roman Republic and then transformed it into the Roman Empire. We must now ask ourselves whether there is something in the notion of "empire" that is independent of the conceptualizations undertaken, at different times and for different purposes, by orators, court poets, clerical scribes, or other propagandists.

The simplest way of tackling this subject is to ask what sort of empire the Pharaohs, or their Hellenistic and Roman successors could have called their own had they been unable to levy tribute from subject populations. If the matter is approached in this crude but realistic fashion, it immediately becomes clear that at least *one* answer to the question has to do with the manner in which surplus wealth is pumped out of conquered regions for the benefit of the imperial metropolis. Nor was this circumstance originally concealed or denied; it was only with the official adoption of Christianity by the increasingly desperate rulers of the declining Roman Empire that a certain degree of hypocrisy was imposed upon the last of the Caesars. On the other hand, it can be argued that the Holy Roman Empire of the German Nation—to give it its official title—came into existence not as an exploitative power, but rather as a defensive reaction on the part of the Catholic Church and the Frankish kingdom, with which the Church had allied itself in the eighth century of the Christian era. The principal enemy then was Islam, at least from the standpoint of the Church, and to that extent the issue was "ideological," to employ the vocabulary of a later age. But it was also highly practical, for the rise of Mohammedan power in the East had disrupted the ancient unity of the Mediterranean civilization, including its economic infrastructure. The Empire, nominally ruled from Constantinople (Byzantium), depended for its material existence upon naval control of the seas that linked its scattered dominions.[2] The Arab conquest in the East and the Germanic inroads in the West posed a twofold problem. If these invaders were converted to some species of the Christian faith, they could be integrated into the crumbling fabric of what had once been the Roman Empire. By the same token, they would cease to be a standing menace to the Pope at Rome and the Emperor at Byzantium. The experiment succeeded with the Germans, but failed with the Arabs, who possessed a rival faith—Islam. The Romano-Germanic kingdoms in the West were gradually brought under Papal control and became the basis of a new European civilization which retained Latin as its official language; it was an economically primitive structure and thus not vitally dependent upon the ancient Mediterranean trade routes. Byzantium and Islam, on the other hand, entered upon a prolonged course of warfare because the Arabs, unlike the Germans, would not give up their faith. Their adherence to Islam made it impossible to integrate them into the Empire—as the Slavic peoples had been—and the endless succession of religious wars resulting from this mutual hostility ultimately brought about the collapse of Byzantium. These wars also ruined the Arabs and the Persians, making them dependent upon the Turks —who thereupon started a fresh round of hostilities by engaging in permanent warfare against the Christian empires of the Habsburgs and Romanovs.

The compressed recital of these familiar facts is intended to bring out a point often lost from sight in contemporary discussions of imperialism: the interplay of "practical" and "ideological" factors, or, to employ less foolish language, the dialectic of being and consciousness. *Prima facie* there was no reason why the Church should have succeeded with the Slavs and Germans, and thereupon failed with the Arabs. The difference lay in the fact that the Arabs possessed a national religion they were unwilling to give up. This circumstance was to determine the course of ten centuries of history. Specifically, it resulted in the alliance between the Holy Roman Empire and the Papacy, with Byzantium increasingly thrown on the defensive and finally going down before the Turkish assault. Unless this historical sequence is taken into account, the whole subsequent course of European history must remain mysterious.[3]

When we ask what the word "Europe" means, we do not, in the first place, inquire into geography. Greece has by some historians been called "the first Europe," for reasons clearly having nothing to do with its location. Inversely, what is nowadays called Europe did not suggest anything remotely civilized to either the Greeks or the Romans. They associated it not with the beautiful Europa of Greek mythology—the lady carried away by Zeus to Crete, where she bore him children—but with barbarous tribes somewhere north of the Danube. The Roman Empire was never European in the later sense of the word. It was Mediterranean, and its civilized rulers entertained the utmost contempt for the savage tribesmen who battered against its frontiers on the Rhine, the Danube, and in Britain. The Byzantine emperors maintained this attitude, and so did their Moslem successors—to their ultimate undoing once "Europe" had become powerful and civilized. For centuries it was neither, even though its medieval rulers eventually taught themselves to read Latin. Nor was there any territorial entity which at first glance could have been perceived as European: geographically, Europe is simply a peninsula of Asia. Historically, it was a latecomer which came into being when the Roman Church entered into a symbiosis with the Germanic tribes, especially the Franks. France is the true heart of Europe and always has been. Its conversion to Roman Catholicism in the sixth century made possible the subsequent rise of the Carolingian Empire and thus set the course of what in later ages was to be called European history. In Roman times there was no such thing. "Europe, in any other sense than an area of land and water, of hills and valleys, plains, mountains, rivers, lakes and forests, did not exist at the beginning of what we usually call European history—that is to say, the history of post-classical times."[4]

The relevance of these circumstances to our theme is once again determined by the peculiar inheritance of Rome, as transmitted by the Roman Church to the post-imperial age of European medievalism. In the transition from the *Imperium Romanum* to the Holy Roman Empire of the European Middle Ages, the crucial fact was the alliance between the Papacy and the kings of France and Germany. The head of the Roman Empire, the *Imperator,* had by late Roman times become the patron of the Church, and the latter returned the compliment by sanctifying the Empire as "eternal." When the barbarian invasions put an end to Rome's eminence, its residual claims to glory were transferred by the Popes to the Carolingian Empire, whose Christian rulers now came to rival the Byzantines as claimants to the succession of the city from which the Empire had once taken its origin. "It is in this double meaning that the Imperium was eulogized as an eternal institution by the Christian Church. And it is in this institutional meaning that the concept was reinterpreted when kings from the North were crowned emperors by the popes in Rome."[5] Having survived the ancient *imperium,* whose culture and traditions it embodied—albeit in a barbarized form—the Church gave birth to a new imperial structure, different from the old in its social composition and in its geographic focus, now shifted from the Mediterranean to northern Europe, but no less extensive in its claims. So far from being merely, in Hobbes's well-known phrase, "the ghost of the Roman Empire, sitting crowned upon the grave thereof," the Church was the active begetter of an entirely new and highly original construction: the *sacrum imperium* of the imperfectly Romanized Franks, with its political capital strung out along the Rhine and its spiritual center in Rome. This new Christian Empire validated its claims to legitimacy by fighting heretics and unbelievers—the Scandinavian Vikings before their conversion, but above all the

Moslems and eventually also the Byzantines and their Eastern Orthodox supporters. The Papacy was a European power and a pioneer of what in later ages was termed "European colonialism." Having converted the Normans and conquered Sicily with their help, it tried to recover Palestine from the Moslems, and it sponsored the first phase of the lengthy *Reconquista* which was to win back Spain for Catholicism. It also supervised the more or less forcible Christianization of the Slavs in Central Europe, which in turn became a factor in the Germanization of these lands.

All in all, the *sacrum imperium* deserves a place in any consideration of what is meant by "imperialism," especially if, employing the German term *Kaiserreich* to denote the "Roman Empire of the Germans," one grasps its full scope and thrust. Hitler was merely the last in a long succession of German-Austrian rulers whose political ambitions centered upon the *Kaiseridee*—the idea of reviving the Carolingian Empire: at the expense of Germany's neighbors, needless to say. But the Russian Czars entertained similar ambitions, although they inherited them from Byzantium. The French and Spanish kings at times likewise toyed with the notion of turning the *sacrum imperium* into a legitimation of *their* imperial ambitions: with Papal help if possible, without the Pope's assistance if necessary. Nor did the Protestant Reformation put an end to these imperial enterprises. On the contrary, one of its indirect, but important, consequences was a prolonged conflict between Spain and England for predominance in America, and the consequent rise of the British Empire.

At first glance, this imperial procession may look rather arbitrary. When some Anglo-Saxon scribes in the earlier Middle Ages first hit upon the idea "that their kings deserved imperial honors, apparently because they had triumphed over the Danes and unified Britain,"[6] they were surely doing no more than might be expected from patriotic writers with vague notions of what the term *imperium* had once portended. But the ease with which republics and kingdoms laid claim to the imperial title, upon every suitable and unsuitable occasion, ought to give one a little pause. Clearly there was something in the dignity that appealed to the imagination of men brought up on the classics, but there was also a sound political reason for styling oneself emperor: it diminished the claims of rival aspirants. Germany was unified by kings who were crowned emperor by the Pope, and in all probability it could not have been unified in any other manner. The Pope in turn, by offering the imperial crown to a German ruler, struck an alliance with that ruler against the Emperor in Byzantium, whose successors would then turn to the Slavs as a counterweight to the Germans. In this manner, imperial, national, and clerical rivalries all intermingled. Or one may say that the imperial title became the legitimation of what purported to be a Christian empire. In a later age, after the religious division brought about by the Reformation, the Protestant rulers of England stood out against the Catholic King of Spain, who by sheer coincidence happened to be both Emperor of Germany and chief claimant to the riches of America. When Elizabeth confronted Philip II and the Armada, she was hailed as the defender of the faith by Protestants unaware of her lukewarmness in theological matters, but she also stood out as a good English patriot and a patron of Francis Drake's successful raids on the Spanish Empire. Less than a century later, Oliver Cromwell fought the Catholic Irish in the name of religion and the Spaniards in the interest of Britain's growing overseas trade. He did not style himself king, let alone emperor, but he inaugurated modern imperialism all the same.

The Elizabethan interlude is of interest because it represents a link between the older and the newer meanings of the term "empire." The *sacrum imperium* of the Germanic Middle Ages rested upon political arrangements ultimately designed to provide the Church with a political armature. In the post-medieval age, the Holy Roman Empire began to look antiquated just because it was more than a purely political contrivance reducible to nation-state exclusiveness and the championship of commercial interests. It raised theological issues, had the See of Rome for its real center, and laid implicit claim not merely to greatness but to quasi-eternity. When the Pope, on a famous occasion, invoked his right to depose the Emperor, he instructed the German princes that it was their duty to elect a king who would do "what was necessary for the Christian creed and for the salvation of the whole *imperium*."[7] After the Renaissance and the Reformation had done their respective work, such claims were no longer admitted even in those parts of Europe that remained Catholic. The kings of France and Spain took good care to make sure that no Pope could depose them as long as they stayed nominally within the faith. In Britain, where the *sacrum imperium* of the Germans had always been something of a joke, Protestantism rendered Papal claims wholly illusory and even made it treasonable for British subjects to take guidance from Rome. In this respect at least, the Renaissance prepared the way for the Reformation. The Italian humanists had already secularized the concept of *imperium* to signify no more than the power to command, which was what it had originally meant to the Romans before the Church lawyers went to work on it. From this it followed that any state with an extended territory might call itself an *imperium* if its rulers so desired. The Italian city-states, where Renaissance humanism flourished, were in no position to make use of this discovery, but the new European nation-states had fewer inhibitions. Their kings stood ready to call themselves emperors at the drop of a crown. If *imperium* signified no more than sovereign authority to rule, why then should the king of England not style himself *imperator?* This was just what Henry VIII did when, in 1532, he entered upon his celebrated quarrel with the Pope. His crown, inherited from no less a dignitary than Constantine, was "imperial." So at least his lawyers affirmed, on the authority of the noted historian Polydore Vergil, and his parliaments dutifully agreed. Scholars might differ on the topic, especially if they were Continentals. "The English

Imperial Crown won firm recognition, indeed, in England—and later on in Great Britain—but it was by no means accepted in the world."[8] No matter. Once the English had been won over to the idea, Elizabethan patriotism in the next generation rallied behind the Protestant queen who inherited Henry's titles as well as his dominions. For good measure, Shakespeare popularized the notion for all time: his England, like his France, was "an Empery."

Ideological delusion? But what force other than patriotism could keep England going during the long years of war against the mighty Spanish Empire? And if the new nationalism clothed itself in ideological forms, political realism raised its head in the writings of Bacon, whose political essays implicitly foreshadowed England's coming "imperial" greatness by stressing the importance of sea power.[9] The term *l'empire de la mer* was also familiar to Bacon's French contemporaries (who may have borrowed it from Virgil's *Aeneid*), though the Dutch jurist Hugo Grotius argued that no state could lay claim to dominion of the seas—there was none *"qui mari imperaret."* In France, there was some uncertainty as to whether Louis XIV ruled an *empire* or a mere *royaume,* but the French Academy eventually laid down the law on this as on most other subjects. Its lexicographers had originally defined an *empire* as a state composed of many peoples, a *royaume* as connoting a political entity expressive of *"l'unité de la nation dont il est formé."* But in 1718 pride got the better of them, although by then the Sun King had departed and been replaced by a mere Regent. In the third edition of their dictionary, they stated that if a kingdom were sufficiently great, it might be called an empire: there was, they affirmed, an *Empire François.*[10]

All this may appear trivial by comparison with what was "really" happening: the rise of the nation-state and the concurrent spread of European power overseas, to Africa, Asia, and America. In fact, all these changes were interlinked, for the new absolute monarchy was the principal vehicle of "imperial" conquest. This circumstance was veiled by internecine conflicts among the European states, which made it difficult to grasp the essential uniformity of what was happening to all of them. Since the *sacrum imperium* had failed to unify Europe—had indeed never seriously tried—it would have seemed absurd to Europeans of the period to identify the acquisition of colonies abroad with "empire" in the Roman sense. European unity, such as it was, appeared as a precarious balance of rival states.[11] Most of them were constantly at war with each other; they also excluded one another from their respective shares in the lucrative African slave trade, which they shared with the Moslems. Yet from a different viewpoint, European power was flowing into regions hitherto untouched by the traditional struggle between the multinational *Respublica Christiana* and the rival "empire" of the Turkish sultans, successors to the Byzantine emperors as well as to the earlier Arab rulers of the Islamic community. It all depended on the meaning one gave to *imperium*. If it simply denoted political sovereignty, then the world was full of kingdoms which might style themselves empires if they had attained a certain magnitude. If the term stood for the more or less forcible unification of different lands, or "crowns," then some kingdoms were empires, others not. Was Britain an empire? The Crown lawyers in the sixteenth century, trying hard to uphold the dignity of their king against Rome, had made such an affirmation—even though England had yet to acquire colonies outside Europe. But it was not until the seventeenth century that the term was to acquire its modern meaning.

The gradual emergence of what in later years was to be known as the British Empire had its roots in domestic affairs, if the subjugation of the Irish can be included under this head. For Henry VIII, the affirmation that "this realm of England is an Empire" constituted part of his struggle to make himself independent of the Pope. Under Elizabeth, who succeeded him after a brief Catholic interregnum, England's power was solidly implanted in Ireland—the first English colony—but the formal union with

Scotland would take another century. Its gradual accomplish-
ment—the result of a lengthy process occurring simultaneously
with the constitutional struggle dramatized by the civil war
between king and parliament and the Cromwellian dictatorship
that succeeded it—gave rise to the concept of "Britain," as
distinct from "England." That is to say, the "British Empire" was
originally perceived as denoting the union of England, Scotland,
Wales, and Ireland: the last-named by conquest, colonization,
and the continuing use of force, since the Irish obstinately re-
fused to abandon their Catholic faith and took every opportunity
to massacre the English and Scottish colonists who had implanted
themselves forcibly on Irish soil. The dual meaning of "empire"—
as the union of different nations under one sovereign and as the
armed subjugation of conquered peoples—was present from the
start, just as it had been in the days of the *imperium*.

Overseas conquest in the newly discovered regions of Asia,
Africa, and America was the next step. Pioneered by Elizabeth
and continued under Cromwell, this mercantile expansion later
became the special province of the Whig aristocracy, which
gained power in the "Glorious Revolution" of 1688. But the
decisive step had already been taken by Cromwell: another
Protestant hero, conqueror of the Irish and mortal foe of Catholic
Spain. Thus at every step political and ideological motivations
intermingled; or rather, religion became the prime vehicle of
imperial expansion. It was not a matter of making the natives
part with their land in exchange for the Bible: this kind of
cynicism belongs to a later age, when religion was no longer taken
seriously and had become the province of missionaries. To the
contemporaries of Elizabeth, the struggle against Catholic Spain
was a life-and-death matter, for defeat would have signified the
extinction of England as an independent entity. Hence the naive
patriotism of Anglican divines who then as later sanctioned wars
of conquest in the name of religion. Hence, too, the ease with
which, from the Reformation to the Civil War of 1642–49 and
the Whig revolution of 1688–89, the idea of a distinctive "British

Empire" fused with the claims of nationhood and Protestantism, to the point where the English came to think of themselves as successors to the lost tribes of Israel. The constitutional quarrel between the Stuart kings and their parliaments, which makes up most of the political history of the century after James VI of Scotland had been proclaimed Elizabeth's heir in 1603, never seriously threatened the fusion of Protestant English nationalism with British imperialism. The folly of the last Stuart king, who tried to reverse this process, cost him his throne, for by then the ruling oligarchy, which had survived Cromwell, was already sufficiently powerful to make and unmake kings. Cromwell, who had established the "Commonwealth of England, Scotland and Ireland, and the dominions thereunto belonging" in 1654, did not create the British Empire. He merely fused an already existing imperial sentiment with the republican principles of the victorious Puritan party. The subsequent defeat of this party, and its later revival on American soil, form part of the history of Anglo-American politics and religion. But its defeat did not alter the imperial thrust. The process of imperial expansion went on steadily all along, under monarchy and republic alike. The urge for "promoting the Glory of God and the Gospel" was indeed peculiarly Cromwellian, but when Puritanism faded out in England, other motivations were readily available to take its place—patriotism above all. They were no less sincerely felt for being in large measure self-serving.[12]

Cromwell made the decisive break, for it was during his rule that the popular ferment let loose by the events of 1640–60 was transformed into the ideology of a new ruling stratum. He did for Puritanism and the English Revolution what Stalin three centuries later accomplished for Bolshevism and the Russian Revolution: he nationalized them. It was not merely that he won out over the Levellers and other radicals who took republican democracy seriously. More to the point, he transformed his military dictatorship into imperialism in the classical sense of the term.[13] The sanguinary reconquest of Ireland from its na-

tive "Papists" (who had been solidly royalist during the Civil
War of 1642–49, hence deserved to be massacred by English
Protestants) was still in the traditional manner. What really
made a difference internationally was the Navigation Act of 1651,
whereby the new republican government laid down the principle
"that the colonies . . . should be subordinated to Parliament,
thus making a coherent imperial policy possible; and that trade
to the colonies should be monopolized by English shipping. As
modified in 1660, the act laid the basis for England's policy
during the next century and a half."[14]

The Navigation Act led straight to the wars against Protestant Holland, the first of which broke out in 1652, while Cromwell was at the height of his power. In plain terms, the war pitted
English Protestant republicans, recently victorious in a civil war
with the Stuart king and his Irish Catholic allies, against Dutch
Protestant republicans: the stake was Britain's overseas trade.
That, of course, was not how the matter was put by the men in
charge of the regicide Republic who in 1649–51 embarked upon
the military conquest of Scotland and Ireland. As they saw it,
the Republic needed a navy to protect itself both from the
royalist fleet commanded by Prince Rupert and from Spain.
Having assembled a fleet, and then discovered in Admiral Blake
a naval commander who was a match for the royalists, they next
proceeded to settle accounts with England's Dutch competitors.
In private, Cromwell regretted the disagreeable necessity of
fighting fellow-Protestants. He would have preferred to fight
Spain instead—and did so on the first suitable occasion, to the
great delight of the godly. But the Dutch were in the way. The
Navigation Act had hit them hard, and war followed in the wake
of commercial rivalry. The Anglo-Dutch struggle was to continue even after Charles II, under the distinguished patronage
of Louis XIV, returned from exile in 1660. Religion, though
still an important consideration, was seen as but one among
others. Empire counted for at least as much. "The Dutch wars
(1652–74) broke the Dutch hold on trade in tobacco, sugar, furs,

slaves, and codfish, and laid the foundation for the establishment of English territorial power in India. English trade to China also dates from these years."[15]

This was not quite the end of the matter. In 1688, James II, who had succeeded Charles, forfeited the throne by his religious folly, and the Whig oligarchy imported William of Orange from Holland to replace him—thereby incidentally inaugurating a hundred-years war against France for control of America and India. For the Dutch, who made possible the Glorious Revolution of 1688, this was a notable revenge, but the triumph was more symbolic than real. "Dutch William" might style himself king of England, but Holland had for all practical purposes become a British protectorate, and the prolonged struggle waged by the Whig oligarchy against Louis XIV and his successors witnessed the steady decline of Dutch power and independence. Nonetheless, the Anglo-Dutch alliance held until the French Revolution a century later introduced a totally new line-up and even transformed Dutch republicans into ardent admirers of France. As long as the Versailles of the Bourbons was associated with absolutism and bloody persecution of Protestants, Holland could not well do anything but seek shelter under the protective shield of British sea power—even at the cost of losing much of its former empire to its successful rival. Protestantism was the faith of the Dutch burghers, and the burgher class looked to the England of Whig parliaments and German-Protestant kings to protect it from the French menace. If New Amsterdam became New York, that was too bad, but bigger issues were at stake: the survival of Holland as an independent country and the physical existence of the Dutch *bourgeoisie,* a class which had reason to fear the triumph of Catholic absolutism. It took the French Revolution to lay this particular ghost. During the century preceding it, the Whig oligarchy had an easy time: England stood for Protestantism, parliamentary government, and progress. Could anyone deny it? Voltaire and Montesquieu could not, and their nagging criticism of the *Ancien Régime* heralded its demise.

But it was the Seven Years' War (1756–63) that really tipped the scales. In the course of that epic conflict, the British swept the French out of India and North America, while Protestant Prussia victoriously stood off the assault of the mighty Austrian and Russian empires. Truly, Protestantism and progress marched together.[16]

Such notions, needless to say, were unwelcome to the Catholic rulers of the great continental European monarchies, but they were not confined to Whig oligarchs and Dutch republicans: Charles XII of Sweden and Frederick of Prussia emphatically concurred. Generally speaking, the fashionable identification of Protestantism with capitalism—especially plausible, for good reason, to Americans—runs up against the stubborn facts of history. Lutheran Sweden and Prussia (the latter admittedly long governed by Calvinist rulers) were military monarchies, not merchant republics, and foreign trade was marginal to their survival as distinctive entities during the wars that marked their emergence on the scene. Sweden acquired an empire of sorts in the Baltic *after* it had, thanks to the efficiency of its army, come to the forefront and engaged in constant warfare with rival powers—some of them fellow-Protestants. Prussia under Frederick never bothered about maritime claims; he left all such matters to his allies, the British. What he wanted and got was Austrian and Polish territory, not colonies overseas. Yet the rise of these absolute monarchies in northwestern Europe, in an age when Spain and Portugal sank into decadence, does seem to have been related to the aftereffects of the Reformation. Conversely, the territorial spread of the rival Austrian and Russian empires in the eighteenth century was evidently a function of their superior military efficiency when compared to the declining Ottoman Turkish Empire, at whose expense Vienna and Petersburg systematically embarked upon conquest. Thus the imperial mystique, once associated with the ancient concept of Christendom, continued to furnish a justification for the great continental empires of the Habsburgs and the Romanovs, while to the west an "Empire of the Sea" was slowly taking shape: pioneered by the Dutch, later taken over by the British, ultimately inherited by their American colonies. France was somewhere in the middle, uneasily perched between two stools, being both an absolute military monarchy ruled by Catholic kings and a maritime power with extensive possessions overseas. These were ultimately lost because the *Ancien Régime* fell into decrepitude, thereby bringing on the Revolution that was to change the face of European politics. Speaking generally, absolutism everywhere acted as the pacemaker of nationalism at home and imperialism abroad. Although hampered by its feudal origins, the absolute monarchy gradually evolved something like a modern consciousness, the centralized state conferring upon its subjects not merely the unsought benefits of taxation and conscription, but also the awareness of forming a separate nationhood. The "forty kings who in a thousand years made France" were no mere figment of royalist imagination. They, and their fellow-rulers elsewhere, did lay the basis of the nation-state.[17]

Did they also pioneer the growth of "imperialism" in the modern sense of the term? Since at the start they presided over precapitalist economies, they cannot well be supposed to have done so. Yet the empire of the Habsburgs and of their Russian rivals grew steadily at the expense of Turkey, and the rulers of Moscow also began that systematic encroachment upon Chinese territory which was later continued from St. Petersburg (and still later, if we are to believe the literature currently issuing from Peking, by the postrevolutionary successors of the Czars). In the end, the answer to the question depends upon the meaning we are prepared to give to the key term. If empire signifies domination over conquered peoples, then the notable differences between Protestant Europe and Counter-Reformation Europe shrink into insignificance. If one is determined to make imperialism rhyme with capitalism, one will have to ignore all empires save those that were built overseas by the nation-states of Western Europe in the age of their maritime predominance. Empire then denotes what was undertaken by the Portuguese, the Spaniards, the French, the Dutch, the British, and finally the Americans. This is the currently fashionable use of the term. It has never made much sense to Germans or East Europeans, and all the evidence suggests that it no longer makes sense to the Chinese either.

Notes

1. Richard Koebner, *Empire* (New York: Grosset & Dunlap, 1965), p. 19.
2. Henri Pirenne, *Mohammed and Charlemagne* (New York: Meridian Books, 1957), pp. 75 ff.
3. *Ibid.*, pp. 147 ff. Bernard Lewis, *The Middle East and the West* (Bloomington, Ind.: Indiana University Press, 1964; London: Weidenfeld & Nicolson, 1968), pp. 16 ff.
4. Geoffrey Barraclough, *European Unity in Thought and Action* (Oxford: Basil Blackwell; New York: Hillary House, 1963), p. 5. For details, see Pirenne, *Mohammed and Charlemagne*, pp. 45 ff.; Heinz Gollwitzer, *Europabild und Europagedanke* (Munich: C. H. Beck, 1964), *passim*. Dieter Groh, *Russland und das Selbstverständnis Europas* (Neuwied: Luchterhand, 1961), *passim*.
5. Koebner, *Empire*, p. 19.
6. *Ibid.*, p. 24.
7. *Ibid.*, p. 28.
8. *Ibid.*, p. 55.
9. *Ibid.*, p. 58. For the general background to the period, see Christopher Hill, *Society and Puritanism in Pre-Revolutionary England* (London: Secker & Warburg; New York: Schocken, 1964), *passim*. Also, the same author's *Puritanism and Revolution* (London: Secker & Warburg, 1958; New York: Humanities Press, 1959), pp. 123 ff. and H. R. Trevor-Roper, *Religion, the Reformation and Social Change* (London: Macmillan, 1967; New York: Harper & Row, 1968), pp. 46 ff.
10. Koebner, *Empire*, p. 60.
11. Barraclough, *European Unity in Thought and Action*, p. 28.
12. Koebner, *Empire*, pp. 61 ff.; Christopher Hill, *Reformation to Industrial Revolution: A Social and Economic History of Britain, 1530–1780* (London: Weidenfeld & Nicolson, 1967; New York: Pantheon, 1968), pp. 20 ff.

13. Christopher Hill, *Oliver Cromwell 1658–1958* (London: Routledge, 1958), *passim*.

14. Hill, *Reformation to Industrial Revolution*, p. 123.

15. *Ibid.*, p. 124.

16. Koebner, *Empire*, pp. 65 ff. James Harrington, who during Cromwell's reign stood on the left wing of the republican coalition, was also among the prophets of the new age. His "Commonwealth of Oceans" was the rhetorical counterpart of Cromwell's attempt to found a maritime empire, even though Harrington was no Puritan and his political ideas were derived from Bacon and Machiavelli. See his *Oceana and Other Works* (1656). It is irrelevant that Harrington was critical of Cromwell's foreign policy, or that, to cite Koebner once more, "the name of the British Empire had no place in the Puritan Commonwealth." *Empire*, p. 67. What matters is that the Cromwellians overcame their scruples to the point of fighting Holland for control of the seas, when in the name of religion they ought to have shrunk from such a godless enterprise. Once the break was made, the "Empire of the Sea," for which the Republic strove, encountered no further ideological resistance, save from those religious and political radicals who had already broken with Cromwell on the issue of democracy.

17. Elie Kedourie, *Nationalism* (1960; rev. ed., London: Hutchinson, 1961; New York: Praeger, 1962); Alfred Cobban, *The Nation State and National Self-Determination* (London: Collins, 1969; New York: T. Y. Crowell, 1970), pp. 23 ff. V. G. Kiernan, "State and Nation in Western Europe," *Past & Present*, no. 31 (July, 1965): 20 ff. For a critique of Max Weber's well-known thesis concerning the relationship of Calvinism to capitalism, see Gabriel Kolko, "Max Weber on America: Theory and Evidence," in *Studies in the Philosophy of History*, ed. George H. Nadel (New York: Harper & Row, 1965), pp. 180 ff.

CHAPTER 4

Empire of the Sea

No ADEQUATE HISTORICAL OR THEORETICAL ARGUMENTS can be assigned for limiting the terms "empire" and "imperialism" to one particular form of domination over conquered peoples, let alone to overseas colonization prompted by mercantile interests. Nonetheless, the present chapter will for convenience be concerned with the British Empire and its American successor. We therefore take as our starting point the "Empire of the Sea," built up during the eighteenth century by the Whig oligarchy which had taken over from the Puritan Commonwealth and the Stuart kings. This approach makes it possible to integrate the principal socio-economic features of the age—mercantilism and colonialism—within the familiar historical perspective that opens with the Whig revolution of 1688–89 and terminates with the French Revolution a century later. The American War of Independence, toward the close of this period, exhibits all the features of a national rising, with the obvious proviso that the revolutionaries were not "underprivileged" helots, but the ruling class of a society largely sustained by slave labor, and, for the rest, free farmers owning their land. In this sense, it was a "bourgeois" revolution, and its aims did not call into question the Whig doctrines elaborated in England a century earlier: an elementary verity adequately attested to by the fact that the official philosopher of Whiggery, John Locke, could be quoted in support of the principles invoked against the imperial British Government in 1776.

In adopting this approach we follow the logic of the economic historians, and this circumstance itself constitutes a novelty. The preceding chapter dealt largely with the tension between medieval and modern forms of political rule, Protestantism being enlisted on the side of modernity, albeit with a few backslidings. The conflicts which determined the rise of England and the decline of Spain were fought out "in ideological forms," the two parties respectively championing the principles of Reformation and Counter-Reformation. During the mercantilist age, which for our purpose begins with Cromwell's Navigation Act of 1651, the rivalries between the European powers cease to be determined by religious antagonisms, although these do not disappear. Political alignments increasingly cut across religious barriers, a circumstance already noticeable during the later stages of the Thirty Years' War (1618–48), when Catholic France and Protestant Sweden allied themselves against the Habsburg Empire. The "end of ideology" aspect of mercantilism is important for our theme, but one must beware of supposing that what became true then had always been the case. We have already seen that neither the medieval nor the early modern period can be satisfactorily explained on the assumption that all parties were concealing crude material interests behind religious professions. What originally occurred in medieval Europe was that the nations constituted themselves in and through religious wars because religious belief defined national identity. When the nation-state finally emerged, it became possible to do without religious uniformity, but this was promptly replaced by a newcomer: patriotism, the affirmation of unquestioning faith in one's country.

A related misunderstanding to be avoided is the notion that in passing beyond feudalism and absolutism one form of interest conflict was simply exchanged for another: war over colonial

spoils for war over territory. It is true that the typical mercantilist conflict had to do with overseas trade and colonies, the
latter furnishing raw materials (and slave labor) for the benefit
of the former. But the ability to discriminate clearly between
economic and noneconomic goals was just what made this new
age so different from the one it succeeded. Feudalism as a system
of government knew no such clear-cut distinction. Its wars—when
not fought against religious heretics or unbelievers—were primarily waged for the purpose of bringing territorial barons under
the control of the central power. The absolutist state which grew
out of this struggle was in the first place an instrument for en-
abling the king to keep his barons in check, and, secondly, a
means of keeping rival kingdoms at bay. So far as its rulers had
economic aims, they were subordinated to the overriding need
for instituting the modern state with all its attendant claims to
sovereignty and popular loyalty. A fairly typical alignment during the medieval epoch enlisted the urban agglomeration, the
bourg, on the king's side against rebellious nobles. Alternatively,
the city fought for freedom from feudal and monarchical oppression. These medieval class conflicts gave rise to the city-state,
perhaps Europe's most distinctive contribution to political history. The East never saw anything like it, for there theocratic
monarchies strangled civic autonomy along with security of private property. For the same reason, the Orient never developed
a genuine capitalism.[1]

On the assumptions common to theorists since the age of
absolutism—Hobbes being the classic case—the politics of the
mercantilist era offer no particular problem, but this is because
we have come to take it for granted that there is such a thing as
a sovereign state acting primarily in the interest of an economically dominant class. To medieval rulers and theologians, such
a statement would have seemed outrageous nonsense, and as
late as the mid-seventeenth century Hobbes's contemporaries
were duly shocked by his *Leviathan*—whose publication date, by
an agreeable irony, coincided with the Navigation Act of 1651.

Hobbes made explicit what both Cromwell and Charles II were busy teaching their contemporaries: religion had been divorced from statecraft. This separation was not the fruit of intellectual enlightenment alone. It had come about because the sovereign state had at long last emerged from the ruins of feudalism. "The states of the Middle Ages had not been sovereign states in the modern sense of the word; indeed sovereignty in its classical conception had almost completely vanished, except insofar as it survived in the Papal claim to *plenitudo potestatis*. It has been said, with some justice if the term is used in its modern connotation, that the only state in the Middle Ages was the Church. The idea of secular sovereignty only reappeared when the Middle Ages were drawing to their close."[2] The Italian city-states were the first modern political entities to escape from the joint tutelage of the Holy Roman Empire and the Church, but they were too small to bring their sea power to bear in waters other than those of the Mediterranean. Venice and Genoa never evolved into "nations." Spain, France, Holland, and England did, and it was in these new nation-states that absolutism found its intellectual defenders.[3]

What is the connection, though, between absolutism and mercantilism, other than the obvious fact that the sovereign nation-state could and did intervene to protect its traders and, incidentally, to expand its own "sphere of influence" at the expense of commercial rivals? To call the 1651 Navigation Act a mercantilist measure is, after all, to say more than that it had something to do with trade and the interest of merchants. It is to specify a structural whole to which the name "mercantilism" can be given: at any rate retrospectively, for the seventeenth century did not employ the term. The "mercantile system" as described by Adam Smith in *The Wealth of Nations*, published in 1776—another historic date terminating one era and inaugurating another—differed from the laissez faire system favored by the early liberals and their successors in that it involved all governments in the ruinous pursuit of an absurd goal: the unend-

ing accumulation of gold and silver. The supply of money, like
the supply of any other commodity, ought to be regulated by
the laws of the market. That, at any rate, was Smith's view, and
his opinion carried weight. But if it was only a matter of governmental imbecility, why had the system endured for 125 years in
Smith's own Britain, and why was it now about to become the
prime issue in the revolt of Britain's American colonies? For an
answer, one must take a look at the "Empire of the Sea" which
the Whig oligarchy had built up in the course of its strenuous
wars against the France of Louis XIV and Louis XV.

The main question is how far the mercantilist system inaugurated between 1650 and 1660 can be invoked to account for the
evolution of the British Empire in the century and a half following that decade. English foreign trade almost doubled between
1700 and 1780, and then trebled during the next twenty years.
That is to say, it grew relatively slowly until the American
colonies had been lost, and a good deal more rapidly thereafter.
At first sight this seems to bear out Smith's contention that
mercantilism was not merely immoral but also senseless; but one
must remember that the Industrial Revolution got into its stride
only after 1780. Economic historians have also observed that
between 1700 and 1780 there occurred a marked shift away from
trade with Continental Europe to trade with the colonies. Since
the essence of mercantilism lay in the systematic preference extended to British merchants and shippers, it would be hazardous
to assert that government policy had nothing to do with the
growth of exports. British control of the seas dated from the
successful conclusion of the War of the Spanish Succession in
1713. *Rule Britannia* was composed, not accidentally, in 1740,
when England had once more entered upon war against Spain,
soon to be aided by France. Altogether, it seems safe to conclude
that the 1651 Navigation Act laid the foundation for the very
lucrative West Indies trade of the next century; while the War
of the Spanish Succession, by securing for England the *Asiento*—
that is to say, monopoly control over the supply of black slaves

to the Spanish-American Empire—speeded the accumulation of commercial capital in England and in Jamaica. This capital accumulation in turn fed the early Industrial Revolution, which had England for its center. In due course, the profits from industrialization made it unnecessary to lean so heavily on trade with the colonies. It also became possible for Britain to abolish the slave trade without ruinous consequences. All told, *The Wealth of Nations* deserved its success: its publication marked the point at which mercantilism had outlived its usefulness. The system then began to look odious and stupid, but that is the usual fate of socio-economic formations which have lost their rationale.

Smith does not have a great deal to say on the subject of slavery, of which he vaguely disapproved on social and moral grounds alike. It was, he thought, much inferior to free labor in point of productivity, for "though the wear and tear of a free servant be equally at the expense of his master, it generally costs him much less than that of a slave. The fund destined for replacing or repairing, if I may say so, the wear and tear of the slave is commonly managed by a negligent master or careless overseer. That destined for performing the same office with regard to the free man, is managed by the free man himself." Elsewhere he rams home the point that "great improvements" are not to be expected from proprietors who employ slaves for their workmen. "The experience of all ages and nations, I believe, demonstrates that the work done by slaves, though it appears to cost only their maintenance, is in the end the dearest of all. A person who can acquire no property, can have no other interest but to eat as much, and to labour as little as possible." This was to become a staple of abolitionist propaganda among the entrepreneurial middle class, which would scarcely have been impressed by purely philanthropic arguments. As in his condemnation of mercantilism in general, Smith sounded a theme which was bound in time to become popular among his readers because it was confirmed by their experience. He never proposed anything that could not be supported by commonsensible reasoning.

Yet colonial slavery had for centuries made possible the existence of large-scale plantation farming in the West Indies and was to endure for yet a considerable stretch of time in the southern regions of what in 1776 was not yet known as the United States of America.

In giving it as his opinion that English colonial progress in North America up to his time had been principally due to "plenty of good land, and liberty to manage their own affairs in their own way," Smith obliquely sided with the New England farmer against the cotton-growing landlord of the South; but he veiled this circumstance by contrasting "the political institutions of the English colonies" with those of their French, Spanish, and Portuguese rivals, who had been left behind in the economic race because *their* political institutions were less favorable to "the improvement and cultivation of this land." He could not have drawn a similar contrast between Britain's possessions in the Caribbean and their French or Spanish neighbors, since all three rested on slavery and the kind of tyrannical administrative rule that commonly goes with it. British Jamaica was not noticeably more productive than Spanish Cuba or French Guadeloupe. On the contrary, French sugar tended to undersell the British product, which was just why the ownership of these islands became an important issue before, during, and after the Seven Years' War of 1756–63. For the same reason, Smith—writing from the standpoint of an early liberalism already attuned to the advantages of free labor as well as of free trade—made little of the topic, although he showed himself aware that immense profits were derived from sugar plantations and that even tobacco, though less remunerative than sugar, yielded a higher revenue than corn. He dealt briefly with the matter, simply reminding the reader that "both can afford the expence of slave cultivation, but sugar can afford it still better than tobacco." Smith knew the facts, but to his mind tropical plantation farming was a kind of extravagance, which was just what made him a pioneer among the economists of his age.

Historically, however, the wealth derived since the sixteenth century from slave labor in the West Indies constituted a form of primitive capital accumulation without which the subsequent implantation of free, as distinct from servile, labor in America could not have been undertaken by the European governments concerned. Moreover, in enslaving the native Indians throughout Latin America, and in subsequently importing slaves from Africa on an enormous scale to work in Brazil or in the Caribbean, these governments adopted the only course open to them during a primitive stage of colonialism, when servile manual labor was just what was wanted. The classic analysis of this subject in Eric Williams' *Capitalism and Slavery* leaves no doubt that the choice was a rational one from the standpoint of mercantilist economic logic, even though the systematic extermination of millions of Indians by the Spanish *conquistadors* was not. African slave labor was the solution to the colonial problem once the Indian had succumbed to excessive work, or proved refractory from the white man's point of view. Given the presence of fertile soil and of crops such as sugar and tobacco, servile labor was economic, even though, ideally, free European workers might have been preferable had they been available in sufficient numbers. The Negro took the place of the Indian when the latter had died out or otherwise signified his unfitness for the role allotted to him under a system of forced labor. For the Indian slave was inefficient, even if he somehow managed to stay alive. The Spaniards soon discovered that one Negro was worth four Indians. The French and English made the same discovery.

In consequence there grew up, over a period of three centuries, that triangular trade between the continents wherein Europe (and eventually North America) supplied the ships, Africa the human merchandise, and the plantations those tropical products of which the market stood in need. The system lasted because Negro slavery enriched the West Indies, to the point of stimulating economic growth in England and France, less so in Spain. The British, French, and Spanish empires all arose on this

foundation of African slave labor, and could not well have
arisen on any other basis. The whole development sailed under
the patronage of nominally Christian governments and was not
seriously challenged until the French Revolution struck a blow
at it by (temporarily) abolishing both slavery and the slave trade.
When the system finally disintegrated after the Napoleonic Wars,
it did so because Britain by then was in the throes of the Industrial Revolution and the islands of the West Indies had ceased
to matter. Their historic role was played out and they became
a backwater.[4]

What all this meant in terms of human suffering has often
been described, although no description is adequate to the subject. Perhaps it is best to let a modern historian speak:

> Schopenhauer refuted pantheism by pointing out the absurdity
> of any God transforming himself into a world where on an
> average day six million slaves received sixty million blows. In
> the history of Negro slavery the extraordinary thing is the ability
> of the race to survive, though myriads of individuals perished; it
> lacked the faculty which Chinese exiles owed to a more complex
> social evolution of mastering a new environment and rising in it.
> It was the endurance of the African, where other enslaved races
> sank under the white man's burdens, that made him so profitable;
> while his weakness in collective organization in his own land
> made him an easy prey. It warped his masters, Arab or Turk,
> Spaniard or Englishman, as much as it degraded him; it con-
> ditioned western Europe to think of all "native" peoples as
> destined bondsmen.[5]

The repeal of the Navigation Acts in 1848—not accidentally
a year when Western Europe was swept by a wave of democratic
revolutions, while in Britain liberalism and free trade consoli-
dated their hold—terminated an epoch that had lasted for several
centuries. In itself the measure was not aimed at slavery: it
merely completed the ruin of the West Indian monopolists whose
interests were no longer effectively represented in the British
Parliament. In the West Indies, slavery had already gone in
1833; it continued in Cuba, Brazil, and the United States. In

the latter country, it took the Civil War of 1861–65 to get rid of the system. By then, the triumph of liberalism was complete. So was the emergence of industrialism. Both had long outgrown the mercantilist system against which Smith had directed his attack in 1776. Neither could have come into existence without it. Moreover, the notion that imperialism had disappeared along with mercantilism and the slave trade was soon shown up as an illusion. Indeed, mercantilism itself was to find intellectual defenders among the pioneers of a new, post-liberal form of imperialism.

Although Smith specifically exempted the original Navigation Act from his strictures, on the grounds that it had been necessary for England's defense, the general tendency of his argument was to make "the commercial or mercantile system" seem absurd. Its authors, he thought, had confused material wealth with money. The protectionist rejoinder to Smith, inaugurated by Friedrich List and other German economists in the following century, stressed the political aspect of mercantilism: the system, they held, was perfectly rational, even though some of the arguments employed in its defense were fallacious. Its purpose was not to maximize welfare, but to promote the economic and political independence of the nation-state. We shall return to this quarrel when we reach the threshold of the Anglo-German conflict which came to overshadow the first half of the twentieth century. In the present context we may agree that mercantilism did help to provoke the revolt of the American colonies, but it did so in the context of a debate among Americans over the advantages to be derived from the existence of a British Empire on American soil. In the course of this debate, leading American spokesmen such as Benjamin Franklin at first made the Empire the symbol of their faith in the future of British America.[6] Anglo-American relations were disrupted because the imperial government clung to its antiquated behavior, and the parting of the ways became inevitable. The emotional driving forces were imperial arrogance on the British side, national sentiment on the

American. There was no insurmountable clash of interest, but rather a political quarrel exacerbated by the British Government's failure to take American patriotism seriously. That the economic conflict need not have escalated to the point of national separation is evident from the fact that Britain in the next century avoided a similar confrontation with Canada.

This is not to deny that mercantilism worked to the disadvantage of the North American colonies, once their internal development had reached the point where they could compete with the imperial metropolis. Between 1700 and 1770 their population grew tenfold—from 200,000 to 2 million. The market they provided for English industries was important, and it was obviously to the interest of English manufacturers not to allow the growth of American competition. Hence the destruction of the American cloth industry in 1719, and the prohibition in 1750 of new iron works on American soil. Even Chatham, otherwise inclined to make concessions to American wishes, declared that he would not allow a nail to be made in the colonies without the express permission of the British Parliament. In practice all this was disregarded, not only by American smugglers and manufacturers, but also by the British Government—for in 1774 one-third of the British merchant navy was being built in America. But the assertion of sovereignty rankled, and in the end it was this, rather than economic discrimination, which drove the Americans into rebellion. The Irish, with worse grievances, had to bear them because British rule over Ireland could be enforced. In America that rule had, for all practical purposes, been rendered ineffective even before the war started, and the proclamations of the British Parliament were resented for their absurdity as much as for the regulations they were trying to enforce. In this sense, the mercantile system had already broken down before it was destroyed in the course of the American Revolution.

In turning the tables on their former British overlords, the Americans made use of an argument Smith had been among the first to expound. The gravamen of his charge against the ruling class of his day was that the mercantile system, professedly designed to obtain a favorable balance of trade, was in reality advantageous only to a narrow group which carried undue weight in Parliament. Governmental interference did not benefit the nation as a whole; it benefited only the merchant oligarchs at the expense of all the rest, including those industries which were positively damaged by the favors bestowed upon shippers and exporters. Mercantilism in fact was a conspiracy got up for the benefit of monopolists determined to keep foreigners out of the home market, damage Britain's European competitors, and reserve the benefits of colonial trade for themselves. Smith's indignation went so far as to denounce the system as contrary to "nature"—the ultimate sanction available to a philosopher of the Enlightenment. His American readers naturally concurred, since it was one of their aims to break the imperial stranglehold upon the lucrative trade with the Dutch, French, and Spanish possessions in the Caribbean. Yet, having won their independence, the Americans displayed a marked reluctance to adopt the core of Smith's program: universal free trade. Industries were necessary for the United States, and these industries had to be built up behind protective tariff walls if they were to survive foreign competition. America's conversion to economic liberalism occurred only after the United States had become the world's leading industrial producer and was on the way to becoming its leading exporter as well—in part at least at the expense of the British. History has an odd way of repeating itself.[7]

Here a parallel strikes the eye of the beholder writing in the year 1970: the comparison between Holland's place in the scheme of things once the British Empire had been constituted, and Britain's very similar position vis-à-vis America two or three centuries later. Reference has already been made to the manner in which the Whig oligarchy employed its Dutch allies in the struggle against France. In British historical literature, the hero of this particular episode is William of Orange, thanks to whom the Protestant alliance against Louis XIV got under way in 1688 (with Papal blessing incidentally, although this fact is seldom mentioned). Dutch historians have, on occasion, come to different conclusions. The most distinguished of them all in recent times, Pieter Geyl, had this to say about the Anglo-Dutch alliance formalized in 1688:

> At the end of the day the close ties which bound Orange to England . . . proved fatal to the internal politics of the Republic and placed her in bondage to England. The dynastic element of the alliance and the intensification of party strife increasingly paralyzed the hand of the Dutch state and led to the total collapse of the old Republic.[8]

Mutatis mutandis, a similar judgment might have been delivered in 1970 by a British historian pondering the results of his country's growing dependence upon the United States ever since the German menace began to materialize around 1900, and more especially in the desperate years after 1940. The British, like the Dutch before them, had no real option, but to concede this is not to say that the alliance was uniformly beneficial for the weaker party. Alliances rarely are.

But how did this reversal of roles come about? Why was the British Empire at the close of the eighteenth century unable to accommodate the American colonies? Or, failing an accommodation beyond a certain point in time, why did the separation—instead of being peaceful, as in the later stages of British imperial history—take the form of a ruinous war? The moment one raises this question, the debate shifts to the political plane. There simply is no way of demonstrating that the economic interests of the British Government and the North American colonies had become irreconcilable by 1775. What had become intolerable was the state of their political relations. To deduce this circumstance from an underlying clash of material interests is to fall into the crudest kind of economism. Nor does the personal factor explain much. George III notwithstanding, a prolonged war with the American colonies, which gave France an opportunity for revenge after the loss of Canada in 1763, was the last thing the British Government wanted. If it drifted into the very situation it was anxious to avoid—another round in the great Anglo-French duel, with the Americans this time enlisted on the French side—the outcome arose from miscalculation. It was *hubris* that drove the British ministers to the point of overstraining the patience of their American friends, Franklin among them. But *hubris,* although common enough, is not measurable or calculable. As a matter of ordinary commonsense, the imperial government—as Burke did not fail to point out—ought to have abstained from the follies that brought about the war and the separation.

So far as the functioning of the British parliamentary system in that age is concerned, few people would dispute the statement that the definitive study of this topic is to be found in the work of L. B. Namier, notably in the volume first published in 1930 under the title *England in the Age of the American Revolution.*[9] However, two qualifications impose themselves. First Namier's fondness for the parliamentary oligarchy he described with such loving care led him to underrate the importance of the Whig-Tory cleavage and to neglect altogether those plebeian undercurrents which were to surface in the course of the long war against the colonies. His bias also accounts for utterances such as the following: "It is to the honour of British statesmen that they did not heed the warnings of those who looked upon the presence of the French in North America as a useful check on the Colonies—although the view was widely canvassed, and ultimately proved correct. For with the removal of the French, the road to independence, and even to a French alliance against Great Britain, was opened for the Colonies."[10] London really had no choice in the matter if it wanted to eliminate the French menace; and the colonies turned to France only when their leaders discovered that there was no way of obtaining autonomy within the British Empire.

In this matter, Franklin is a better guide than Namier. In the pamphlet already mentioned he predicted that the population of the colonies would double every quarter century and admon-

ished the British Government to secure additional living space
for these newcomers, on the grounds that a prince who "acquires
new Territory, if he finds it vacant, or removes the Natives to
give his own People Room" deserves the gratitude of posterity.[11]
This expansion was in the interest of mother country and colony
alike. "What an Accession of Power to the *British* Empire by
Sea as well as by Land! What Increase of Trade and Navigation!
. . . How important an Affair then to *Britain* . . . and how
careful should she be to secure Room enough, since on the Room
depends so much the increase of her People."[12] At a conference
of governors and colonial representatives held at Albany in
1754, Franklin submitted plans for a federalized Empire. In
1761, toward the close of the Seven Years' War, he sided with
Pitt in urging that the British acquire control of Canada. For
this was the key to the Mississippi valley, which in turn could
be used for "raising a strength . . . which, on occasions of a
future war, might easily be poured down upon the lower country
[presumably Florida] and into the Bay of Mexico, to be used
against Cuba, the French islands, or Mexico itself."[13] All told,
Franklin had a fairly realistic view of the future. This of course
did not prevent the Founding Fathers of the Republic—or the
worthy Thomas Paine, who believed all they told him—from
affirming after 1776 that the "French and Indian wars" of 1689–
1763 had been exclusively the work of the sinful British Government, but for whose constant meddling the American settlers
would have lived in perfect peace with their neighbors and never
coveted an inch of their soil. In the words of the American historian already cited, "they wished to forget the dimly-formed
principle of empire solidarity for which both Pitt and Franklin
stood in 1761, and to chart a new course of empire unhampered
by a distant government."[14] Yet the idea of a federalized British
Empire took a long time to die. It had influential spokesmen in
the Continental Congress of 1774 and it was resolutely cham-
pioned by the leaders of the Whig oligarchy in Britain, Chatham,

Fox, and Shelburne among them. But for the imbecility of George III and the Tory squires who backed his Ministers, it would probably have been adopted as a compromise solution before French intervention, and the growing radicalization of the colonies, had rendered all such schemes illusory. For that matter, the immediate effect of the French alliance in 1778 was to stimulate Congress into an unsuccessful attempt to wrest Canada from the British. America had been launched on its imperial path, from which, in two centuries, it has never swerved.

Nor is there anything surprising about this. The notion that imperial expansion was "natural" formed part of the stock equipment of the Enlightenment. On this point it is unnecessary to go back to Hobbes, let alone Machiavelli, whose primitive schemes for the aggrandizement of his native Florence belong to the city-state era. By the time of the American Revolution, the concept of "empire" had been redefined to embrace the notion of "civilization." When Alexander Hamilton talked of acquiring control of the Caribbean, he did not shock his opponents. "To both of the political parties—Federalists and Republicans—the new federal union was an empire. The two terms were equivalents in the vocabularies of Washington, Adams, Hamilton, and Jefferson."[15] It was not until the Civil War that public men learned to talk of the "American nation" instead. By the time America had completed its purely territorial expansion, it was no longer politic to speak of "empire," a concept associated with the effete British and the European monarchies generally. American democracy would have no truck with the notion of lording it over subject people—until the Spanish-American war of 1898 suddenly precipitated what could no longer be described as anything but "imperialism" in the classical meaning of the term. But it was liberal imperialism—the imperialism of "progress." The United States did not wish to annex foreign countries; it merely desired to improve them for their own good. The aim was no longer continental expansion and the acquisition of territory, but political penetration in the interest of economic development. But then the British had by 1900 reached a similar stage and adopted the same sort of language. Moreover, they were beginning to federalize their Empire—or at least the white-settler parts of it—and to project self-government for India. Liberal imperialism—the imperialism of Gladstone, Lloyd George, Churchill, and the two Roosevelts—was of course not mercantilist and made no attempt to interfere with economic laissez faire. On the contrary, it promoted it; that was the whole point about it.

To be effective, though, this sort of penetration needed a secure home base, whence the Monroe Doctrine and other trifling departures from the principle of nonintervention in the affairs of others. Moreover, the nation-building process developed its own momentum, always threatening to spill over into annexation. This was something the British could have told their American pupils, had they been willing to listen. American expansion was national before it became imperial in the classical sense, but the border line could be crossed even in the age of Jefferson, when the country acquired Louisiana from France in 1803 by purchase and then thought of "liberating" Canada in 1812–14. Was this mere nation-building or something else? The answer depends once more upon the meaning one accords to the term "imperialism." We have all been conditioned of late to identify it with capitalist expansion, and in the era of the Industrial Revolution that is basically what it was. But the story of Russian expansion into Siberia in the seventeenth century and the current dispute between Moscow and Peking serve as reminders that possessions may be acquired by the simple process of pushing into sparsely inhabited territory and replacing the indigenous population by settlers belonging to the dominant people. The notion that an empire must necessarily consist of overseas colonies is a fantasy. This topic will be discussed later. Here we simply note that there is no need to invoke hidden interests as the force behind continental expansion in the nineteenth century. The process of nation-building in North America inevitably involved the United States in rivalry with the empires of Britain and Spain. In this sense of the term, the Republic was "imperial" from the start.

Notes

1. V. G. Kiernan, "State and Nation in Western Europe," *Past & Present*, no. 31 (July, 1965): 23. The statement applies to India and the Islamic world with greater exactitude than to China and Japan, the last-mentioned country at least having developed a genuine feudalism and the notion of personal property in land that commonly goes with it. In China, and still more in India and the Middle East, this development was strangled at birth by the system of government usually described as Oriental despotism. The realization that capitalism could sprout from feudalism in Europe (and subsequently in Japan) only because private property was beyond the reach of a despotic central power, forms the connecting link between Marx's and Max Weber's theorizing. See, among other works, Karl Marx, *Pre-Capitalist Economic Formations*, trans. Jack Cohen and ed. E. J. Hobsbawm (London: Lawrence & Wishart, 1964; New York: International Publishers, 1965), *passim*.

2. Alfred Cobban, *The Nation State and National Self-Determination* (London: Collins, 1969; New York: T. Y. Crowell, 1970), p. 29.

3. For Hobbes's contribution to this topic see Richard Peters, *Hobbes* (London: Penguin Books, 1967; Baltimore: Penguin, 1968), pp. 178 ff.; Leo Strauss, *The Political Philosophy of Hobbes* (Chicago: University of Chicago Press, 1963), *passim;* C. B. Macpherson, *The Political Theory of Possessive Individualism* (Oxford: Clarendon Press; New York: Oxford University Press, 1962), pp. 87 ff.; K. C. Brown, ed., *Hobbes Studies* (Oxford: Basil Blackwell; Cambridge, Mass.: Harvard University Press, 1965), *passim*. It has often been pointed out that Hobbes is "modern"—that is to say, bourgeois—in his approach to politics: he counterposes a mass of atomized individuals to the sovereign state. What is rather more relevant is his failure to make a convincing transition from psychological atomism to political absolutism. On his general assumptions about human nature, if taken seriously, it is by no means apparent why free individuals should contract to establish an absolute power suspended like a sword over their heads. Locke's solution was more closely attuned to the sentiments of the propertied classes in England and America, and he succeeded where Hobbes had failed. But the *Leviathan*

did mark a decisive break with political theology: God was expelled from history and replaced by man's fear of death.

4. For the general theme, see Eric Williams, *Capitalism and Slavery* (London: Andre Deutsch, 1964; New York: Atheneum, 1962), *passim*.

5. V. G. Kiernan, *The Lords of Human Kind: European Attitudes Toward the Outside World in the Imperial Age* (London: Weidenfeld & Nicolson; Boston: Little, Brown, 1969), p. 196.

6. Richard Koebner, *Empire* (New York: Grosset & Dunlap, 1965), pp. 88–89. The reference is to Franklin's *Observations Concerning the Increase of Mankind, Peopling of Countries etc. (1751)*.

7. Adam Smith, *The Wealth of Nations* (New York: Random House, 1937), pp. 402–3: "That foreign trade enriched the country, experience demonstrated to the nobles and country gentlemen, as well as to the merchants; but how, or in what manner, none of them well knew. The merchants knew perfectly in what manner it enriched themselves; it was their business to know it. But to know in what manner it enriched the country, was no part of their business. This subject never came into their consideration, but when they had occasion to apply to their country for some change in the laws relating to foreign trade. It then became necessary to say something about the beneficial effects of foreign trade, and the manner in which those effects were obstructed by the laws as they then stood." Smith's virtuous indignation was perfectly genuine, and perfectly adapted to the situation of a country which had outgrown the swaddling-clothes of mercantile protection and become able to trade on equal terms with all the world. His American pupils two centuries later added nothing to his argument, while subtracting something from his style.

8. Pieter Geyl, *Orange and Stuart 1641–72*, trans. Arnold Pomerans (London: Weidenfeld & Nicolson; New York: Scribner, 1969). From the Dutch original, *Oranje en Stuart*, published in 1939.

9. L. B. Namier, *England in the Age of the American Revolution*, 2d ed. (London: Macmillan; New York: St. Martin, 1961). See also his earlier *The Structure of Politics at the Accession of George III*, 2d. ed. (London: Macmillan; New York: St. Martin, 1957).

10. Namier, *England in the Age of the American Revolution*, pp. 281–82.

11. Richard W. Van Alstyne, *The American Empire: Its Historical Pattern and Evolution* (London: Routledge, 1960), p. 5.

12. *Idem.*

13. *Ibid.*, pp. 5–6.

14. *Ibid.*, p. 7.

15. *Ibid.*, p. 10.

CHAPTER 5

Liberal Imperialism

"1776, AS ALL KNOW, AND IT IS ONE OF THE FEW THINGS that all know, was the year when America declared her independence (4th July) and Adam Smith published the *Wealth of Nations* (9th March) . . . Not so many know, or knowing remember, that on 25th August, 1776, David Hume breathed his last and that in March 1776 Canada repulsed an invasion from America."[1] Mr. C. R. Fay's irony is understandable. He is after all British, and hence inevitably prejudiced against the American Republic. He even compares the American colonists to the Boer settlers who in 1899 made a stand for political independence from the British Empire (ultimately successful, since they scored in the political arena after losing their fight on the battlefields of the South African veld). But we must attend to the theoretical core of this author's argument, since he happens to be an economic historian. The topic which concerns us is the survival of imperialism into the nineteenth century, when by all the standards of free-trade logic it ought to have faded away. Why did imperialism not follow mercantilism into oblivion? Why did it revive and expand at the very peak of the liberal era, in the age of Gladstone, thus giving rise to the phenomenon known in British literature as "liberal imperialism?" These are nagging questions for liberals. They have become equally nagging for socialists ever since it began to dawn on them that socialism was not immune to the infection. For the moment, however, we are concerned with the liberal nineteenth century and the system of economic organization then prevalent in the Western world.

That system, as no one needs to be told any longer, was capitalism. But what kind of capitalism? After all, mercantilism too can be included under this head. At this point, however, we must be clear what we are talking about. If by mercantilism we mean merchant capitalism, that is, capitalism *before* the Industrial Revolution, there is no further problem: everyone can see at once in what sense the nineteenth century marked a watershed. What mattered was no longer colonial trade in sugar and other tropical products grown by slave labor on West Indian plantations, but the output of the new factories serviced by machines and free labor, although cotton grown by slaves for the benefit of textile manufacturers provided a link with the earlier stage down to the American Civil War. Setting aside the American South as an anomaly which somehow survived into the new age, we can draw a clear dividing line between the earlier and the later period: merchant capitalism and slave labor on the one hand, industrial capitalism and wage labor on the other. This is the standard liberal view of the subject, inaugurated by Smith and brought to perfection by Ricardo, Mill, and their successors. It is also substantially the Marxist view. Marx after all was the heir of Ricardo and the contemporary of Mill. The economic system he describes in *Capital* is the mature industrial capitalism of the later nineteenth century.

There exists, however, a somewhat different view of the subject, pioneered by Friedrich List (1789–1846) and brought to perfection by Gustav von Schmoller (1838–1917) and the other writers of the so-called German Historical School. List, an economic nationalist and advocate of industrialization, thought protectionism quite rational and rejected laissez faire as unsuitable for Germany and for Britain's competitors in the nineteenth century generally. It was, he thought, something the British were trying to export, along with cotton, to the detriment of industrially less-developed nations. List's arguments were echoed by his American contemporary Henry C. Carey (1793–1879), and by the latter's German admirer Eugen Dühring, another nationalist and the butt of Friedrich Engels's celebrated tract (1878). Dühring, a fanatical anti-Semite, was to become a major figure in the pantheon of German National Socialism, but we are not obliged to hold List responsible for all his pupils. Most of them were quite respectable, although it is not without interest that Werner Sombart (1863–1941) ended his days as a supporter of Hitler. The early founders of the Historical School (Bruno Hildebrand, Wilhelm Roscher, and Karl Knies) were moderate liberals in their general philosophy, and their successors—principally Schmoller, Karl Bücher, and Lujo Brentano—conserved many elements of the liberal outlook, although Schmoller at least was also an enthusiastic imperialist. We shall come to that presently, but let us stay for a moment with the dispute over the meaning of mercantilism. Schmoller's main theme throughout his career was that economic life depended on political decision-making. There was no such thing as a self-propelling market system geared to the demands of individuals. Rather, the economic process was guided by state action, and always had been: "mercantilism . . . in its inmost kernel is nothing but state-making—not state-making in a narrow sense, but state-making and national-economy-making at the same time."[2]

Schmoller did not dispute Smith's description of how the "mercantile system" actually worked; exports were artificially stimulated by bounties, imports hampered by a ban on foreign manufactures, trade was promoted by commercial treaties, and the colonies were reserved for the imperial metropolis. What was wrong with all that, he asked? It was simply a way of building up the power of one's nation. The wars of the seventeenth and eighteenth centuries had admittedly been trade wars, but then it was perfectly proper and legitimate to advance the cause of one's country at the expense of rivals:

> . . . it was precisely those Governments which understood how to put the might of their fleets and admiralties, the apparatus of customs laws and navigation laws, with rapidity, boldness and clear purpose at the service of the economic interests of the nation and state, which obtained thereby the lead in the struggle and in riches and industrial prosperity.[3]

Schmoller, a prominent academic in the Bismarck era, inevitably sounded rather "Prussian" to British liberals, but he was not without influence in contemporary England, where economic nationalism was reviving under the spur of German competition. William Cunningham, author of an important work entitled *The Growth of English Industry and Commerce,* owed much to Schmoller. Mercantilism, he agreed, could not be dismissed as a conspiracy got up to enrich a few merchants: "Politicians of the sixteenth, seventeenth and the greater part of the eighteenth century were agreed in trying to regulate all commerce and industry so that the *power* of England relative to other nations might be promoted, and in carrying out this aim had no scruples in trampling on private interests."[4]

This view of the subject was not contested in Eli Heckscher's *Mercantilism,* first published in Sweden in 1931 and translated into English three years later. Heckscher was no admirer of what the Germans called *Merkantilismus,* not to mention *Staatsbildung.* He agreed that Schmoller and the other members of the Historical School had described the system correctly, but he condemned its purpose. It was wrong to aim at the extension of state power: the proper goal of economic policy was the creation of wealth; mercantilism was an aberration because of its intermingling of political and economic forces. Fay's work likewise represented a reaction to the school of thought founded by Cunningham; he had no patience with *Merkantilismus* at all:

> I agree, as I have said, with Edwin Cannan that it is a misfortune that the German historical school took hold of the con-

cept of mercantilism and so re-cast it that they provided the fatherland with a place in the mercantile sun. Schmoller's mercantilism not less than Bücher's is an economic bastard. The Germany of the sixteenth, seventeenth, eighteenth, and early nineteenth centuries was, quite as much as Italy, outside the mercantile sweep, whether we are thinking of doctrine, policy, or system of trade. If Germany was mercantilist, then mercantilism is just economic nationalism, and a good word wasted.[5]

Not wasted, however, to the mind of economic nationalists who favored protectionism as against the practice of free trade, triumphant with the abolition of the Corn Laws in 1846, when England was at the peak of its industrial eminence and had no need to fear foreign competition. In this respect, List worked out a system of ideas he had picked up in America from the followers of Alexander Hamilton. His own pupils may have misused the term *Merkantilismus,* but they knew what they wanted.

The final turn of the wheel, ironically enough, is associated with Keynes who, in an Appendix to his *General Theory of Employment, Interest, and Money* (1936), undertook a reassessment of the mercantilists. On balance he found much to praise in their "contribution to statecraft, which is concerned with the economic system as a whole and with securing the optimum employment of the system's entire resources"—an aim in whose pursuit "the methods of the early pioneers of economic thinking in the sixteenth and seventeenth centuries may have attained to fragments of practical wisdom which the unrealistic abstractions of Ricardo first forgot and then obliterated."[6] This heresy brought down upon his head the wrath of Professor Heckscher, but Keynes was unabashed and he had the last word. In November 1946, a century after England's formal conversion to free trade and laissez faire, the Chancellor of the Exchequer in Britain's first postwar Labour Government, Mr. Hugh Dalton, laid it down that "the first principle to be adopted in our export policy [is] to export fully manufactured goods in preference to partly manufactured goods. . . . The more brains and craftsmanship we can export, the better for our balance-of-payments position and thus the higher our standard of living." The wheel had come full circle. Keynes's belated conversion to the view that there was no self-adjusting mechanism of foreign trade, and his statement that in monetary matters "we, the faculty of economists, prove to have been guilty of presumptuous error in treating as a puerile obsession what for centuries has been a prime object of practical statecraft" rang the knell for economic liberalism. It did so, in the words of a later writer, "especially as the suspicion grew that the age of *laissez-faire* had perhaps been an interlude between the mercantile age and what threatened to be another extended period of regulation according to principles not unlike those of the earlier period."[7]

Having stressed the parallel between the old and the new protectionism, we must now emphasize the difference. Heckscher and others drew attention to the chief weakness of mercantilist theorizing: it was not merely nationalist and attuned to the idea of war, but likewise haunted by the notion that the world's total wealth formed a given quantity which could not be significantly increased. From this it followed that a nation could enrich itself only at the expense of its rivals. It was this faulty reasoning that induced the classical economists of the liberal age to treat their forerunners as imbeciles. That they were not justified in doing so was the burden of Keynes's argument in 1936, for he had by then reluctantly come around to the conclusion that the economic system was not self-regulating, and that state intervention was needed to keep it in balance. This did not make him a nationalist, nor did he have to become an imperialist: for Britain already possessed the world's greatest empire.

The Germans before 1914 were in a different position. Having no significant overseas possessions—the African colonies acquired by Bismarck were barely beginning to produce a few raw materials—and feeling hemmed in at home, they came to rest their hopes on the idea of Central European hegemony. From there it was only a step to the idea of "colonizing" the Slavs: the Ukraine was to be their Africa. In this respect, Hitler was merely the executor of a Pan-German program which had begun to take shape in the 1890's. The intellectual justification was provided by the theorists of the Historical School: the earth was about to be divided up among rival empires, and Germany must not be left out. To the classical liberal thesis that the world market was capable of indefinite expansion, there was now a counter-argument: the world's total economic resources might be un-limited, but unless action were taken in time, the great empires would shut out their rivals.

What then were the specifics of German imperial policy before 1914? To answer this question, we must go back to Schmoller. We have not yet finished with this distinguished economic his-torian, for he was very much involved in the question of im-perialism in the age preceding the world wars of the present century. In 1890, when Caprivi—Bismarck's successor from 1890 to 1894—was trying to work out a system for linking the newly founded German *Reich* more closely to its European neighbors and satellites, Schmoller came to his aid with an article boldly forecasting a new age of imperialism, and incidentally giving everyone a foretaste of Germany's war aims in 1914:

> He who is perceptive enough to realize that the course of world history in the twentieth century will be determined by the competi-tion between the Russian, English, American, and perhaps Chi-nese world empires, and by their aspirations to reduce all the other, smaller, states to dependence on them, will also see in a Central European customs federation the nucleus of something which may save from destruction not only the political inde-pendence of those states, but Europe's higher ancient culture itself.[8]

German writers have traditionally excelled in making gloomy forecasts, and they have done so because Hegel taught them to think historically. As early as 1842, Hegel's pupil Bruno Bauer, writing in the liberal *Rheinische Zeitung*, then edited by his friend Marx (not yet a communist), had drawn alarming conclusions from his reading of Tocqueville: "Whoever thinks of Europe's and Germany's future must not overlook North America, for the struggle among the European states will soon give place to a greater conflict, that between continents (*dem Kampf der Welttheile*)."[9]

Where then is the economic link between the old mercantilism and the new imperialism? On this topic Mr. Fay is an unimpeachable witness, being in the English liberal tradition: "Note, first, what the system was. It was a type of imperial economy, the fruit of that overseas (not overland) expansion whereby Holland and England, followed tardily by the other great powers and by Germany last of all, reached imperial stature and economic power."[10] The system was pioneered by the Dutch. The Italian city-states and their German counterparts had missed the boat, while France and Spain were too landlocked, and too busy with the Counter-Reformation, to give their full attention to overseas conquest. Only England was in a position to take up where the Dutch had left off. Holland soon lost its lead, and England lost the American colonies, but by then the break had been made: The "mercantile system," with its roots in urban commerce, had superseded the old agrarian economy of feudal Europe and laid the basis for capital accumulation in the Industrial Revolution which burst upon the global scene around 1850.

But why were the Germans first in rehabilitating the old mercantilist doctrine? The answer should by now be obvious. Imperial Germany was trying to make up for lost time, and in the process it rediscovered some elements of that "practical wisdom" to which Keynes was subsequently to pay reluctant tribute in 1936. The Historical School was not alone in stressing the importance of the state in fostering economic growth: Marx had done the same in *Das Kapital*. But Marx was a heretic, whereas Schmoller and his friends were leaders of opinion in the Germany of Bismarck and William II. All told, they laid the theoretical basis for German policy in the new age of empire-building. In this they were both helped and hindered by their intellectual heritage: helped because they had no need to inflate laissez faire into a world view; hindered because their political conservatism left them with nothing more entrancing to offer their countrymen than self-aggrandizement as a national goal. German imperialism thus got under way *without a universal idea to sustain it,* and this circumstance in the end proved to be its ruin.

How did the British react to the German challenge? In the first place, by ignoring it. This was easy enough during the mid-Victorian era when industrial competition, such as it was, came chiefly from the United States, followed at a distance by France and Belgium who presented no direct military threat. The German Confederation was a ponderous decentralized affair until Bismarck came along, and its rulers generally tended to side with England against France, then the most active imperial rival in Africa and Asia. No problem here, but certain troublesome undercurrents were already beginning to make themselves felt in the heyday of Cobdenite liberalism and Palmerstonian imperialism. In the first place, Cobden's free-trade gospel, while effective enough in the economic sphere, quite failed to restrain either Whigs or Tories when it was a matter of supporting Turkey against Russia by military force (1853–56) or of annexing island territories and colonies abroad. Nor was the bloody suppression of the Indian Mutiny in 1857 exactly in tune with liberal tenets. If England faced rebellion in Ireland or India, the army had to be employed, and the army was officered by the landed gentry, which in turn supported the Tories—as did the Anglican Church, much of the rural population, and a sizable proportion of the urban working class. All very awkward, especially when, in the 1870's, Disraeli invented the "new Toryism": a clever mixture of imperialism abroad and inexpensive social reforms at home. The mixture proved popular, and, by the 1880's, Gladstone's Liberal Party felt obliged to adapt itself to the trend. By then, the mid-Victorian free-trade boom was over, German and American competition was getting stiffer, and laissez faire no longer seemed quite as convincing as it had to the generation of Cobden and Bright. Something had gone wrong. What was it?

First, there was the relative narrowness of the Empire's home base. Britain was an island, and this circumstance afforded obvious strategic advantages, but it also imposed limitations upon the growth of population and the use made of home-based resources. British surplus capital and labor could and did migrate to Canada, Australia, New Zealand, and South Africa, but in the process new and potentially rival nations came into being, even though valuable economic and cultural links were forged at the same time. The financial profit-and-loss account does not tell the whole story. British firms abroad repatriated a proportion of their earnings, and their presence helped to promote the growth of British shipping, banking, and insurance. On the other hand, the metropolis was drained of capital and technical ability for the benefit of what were ultimately foreign countries, albeit English-speaking ones. Who reaped the principal advantage from all this? The British Isles? It was difficult to strike a balance.

> In the literal sense Britain was perhaps never the "workshop of the world," but her industrial dominance was such in the middle of the 19th century that the phrase is legitimate. She produced perhaps two-thirds of the world's coal, perhaps half its iron, five-sevenths of its small supply of steel, about half of such cotton cloth as was produced on a commercial scale, and forty per cent (in value) of its hardware. On the other hand even in 1840 Britain possessed only about one-third of the world's steam power and produced probably something less than one-third of the world's total of manufactures. The chief rival state, even then, was the U.S.A.—or rather the northern states of the U.S.A.—with France, the German Confederation, and Belgium. All these, except in part little Belgium, lagged behind British industrialization, but it was already clear that if they and others continued to industrialize, Britain's advantage would inevitably shrink. . . . By the end of the 1880's the relative decline was visible even in the formerly dominant branches of production. By the early 1890's the U.S.A. and Germany both passed Britain in the production of the crucial commodity of industrialization, steel.[11]

Let us now step back and consider the long-run sequence of "what really happened," as distinct from what the participants imagined themselves to be doing. The crucial issue is the relationship between the old and the new imperialism: that which preceded the Industrial Revolution and that which followed it. After what has been said before about the role of mercantilism, it comes as no surprise to find that the latest scholarly exposition of the topic puts forward an interpretation which combines Marxian and Keynesian insights. Hobsbawm's *Industry and Empire*—like Hill's work (noted in Chapter 2)—centers on the thesis that the earlier British Empire was crucial in promoting the industrial transformation of 1750–1850 which in turn gave rise to the second British Empire: the one that went to war against Germany in 1914 and again in 1939. The theoretical core of the argument may be summarized as follows: the Industrial Revolution could not have occurred in Britain but for the possession of a colonial empire which provided outlets far in excess of anything the home market could absorb. Industrialization entailed a sudden expansion of productive capacity only possible in a country which occupied a key position within the evolving world economy. The decisive factor was a global monopoly of export markets during the difficult transition from a self-supporting economy to one dependent on world trade. This position, in its initial stages, was secured by the conquest of overseas territories in North America and India during the eighteenth century, principally in competition with France. The aggressive wars waged by the British oligarchy between 1702 and 1815—when Napoleon's defeat sealed the close of this chapter—established a universal trade monopoly, notwithstanding the setback caused by the loss of the American colonies. After 1815 Britain ruled the waves and was becoming the world's workshop. In these circumstances, further major annexations were unnecessary, and economic penetration could take the place of military conquest. A country whose industries could undersell those of its competitors was favorably placed to preach the universal adoption of free trade, and so it did—to the detriment of those among its rivals who lacked the wit or the power to set up protective barriers behind which they could themselves industrialize at a pace that suited them. The major European nations and the United States could not be prevented from doing so, but the modernization of India was delayed, and "honorary" dominions such as Argentina entered upon a trade relationship which satisfied their landed oligarchy at the expense of their industrialists. The net effect was to place Britain at the center of an international web resting upon privileged relations with Europe, North and South America, and smaller industrial enclaves in other continents. The peak was reached between 1850 and 1875, when the national commitment to free trade underwrote the social dominance of the industrial entrepreneurs and the preponderance of liberalism. The subsequent grab for Africa, beginning in 1880, was a sign that liberal imperialism had begun to flag. Britain's competitors were fast catching up, and it became necessary once more to lean on the "formal" Empire—India above all, but Egypt and Africa too, so far as they could be controlled. India in particular was the key to the imperial structure: politically (because of the size of the Indian Army) and economically (because the country financed two-fifths of Britain's payments deficit). Laissez faire liberalism was not extended to India, except insofar as its home-grown textile industries were destroyed for the benefit of British exports. In one way or another—through India's own export surplus with China, or through direct Indian payments for the privilege of being governed by Britain—this enormous country thus became the keystone of the imperial arch before 1914. But this imbalance pointed to the fact that, in strictly economic terms, British industry was no longer globally competitive. Possession of India provided a payments surplus secured by politico-military power alone.

Too narrow a home base, then, to sustain a world-wide export monopoly, once Britain's competitors had caught up with or passed her in the all-important domain of modern industry.

During the earlier period Britain had been able to effect the changeover from mercantilism to free trade because the Industrial Revolution gave her a temporary monopoly of the new mode of production. Hence an abnormal reliance upon international trade at the expense of the home market. Hence also the illusion—fed by arguments supplied by the classical economists, from Smith to J. S. Mill—that mercantilism had never been anything but an aberration due to faulty reasoning and accidental political entanglements. The mid-Victorian sense of security rested upon a precarious balance of political and economic factors which enabled the British to have their cake and eat it too: possess an overseas empire while practicing free trade. The British economy being ahead industrially, foreign trade translated itself into an exchange of manufactures and services (shipping, banking, insurance) against primary products (mainly imported food and raw materials). Most of these were not produced by the colonies properly so called, but by autonomous countries, with the United States, Canada, Argentina, and Australia in the lead. The exchange benefited Britain in the measure to which it sustained the consequences flowing from the historical accident of having been first with the Industrial Revolution, but this state of affairs could not last forever. The 1880's were a period of stagnation, with the real income of British workers slowly creeping upward only because the price of imported foodstuffs fell. By the 1890's the issue was in the open: the Americans and the Germans were moving ahead industrially. Not accidentally, this decade witnessed a deep cleavage within the Liberal Party, socialist stirrings among newly unionized workers, and the concurrent growth of an avowedly imperialist movement—that is to say, a movement no longer content with the invisible "imperialism of free trade," but one that called for protective tariff walls to be built around the Empire. Like all such movements, imperialism went in for "protecting the British worker"—at the expense of foreigners, of course. This gave it a populist coloration, badly needed in an age of democracy and parliamentary elections; but it also supplied a rationale for Tory politicians, paternalist employers, imperial proconsuls in retirement, socially-minded clergymen, and sturdy patriots who resented foreign immigrants. They all agreed on one thing: the British worker was hard done by, and the best way to help him was to keep foreigners and their goods out of the country.[12]

The ideology of modern imperialism, and its critique by liberal and socialist writers from about 1900 onward, will be considered in the next chapter. In postponing this topic for the moment, we do not treat it as irrelevant, or as a mere epiphenomenon of the "real" process occurring in the socio-economic sphere. Any such distinction is untenable, for it neglects the all-important connections at the level of political decision-making. State action was mediated by beliefs, more or less rational, concerning the role of the government in promoting what was called "the national interest." The fact that the governing classes everywhere interpreted this interest to suit their own convenience is irrelevant. In a certain fundamental sense the political ideology of every commonwealth is the ideology of its ruling class; but a truth so general as to apply to all recorded history tells us little about the theme under discussion. Nor can the ideology of imperialism be treated as a mere subterfuge, artfully contrived to blind democratic electorates to what was being done behind their backs. The quarrel between the mercantilists and the laissez faire school was fought out in the open. The debate over imperialism occupied an entire generation between 1880 and 1914, and the way in which it shaped European public opinion was itself a factor in promoting the outbreak of war in 1914. We have already seen what was involved in the political commitments of the German Historical School during the Bismarck era, and the topic will once more engage our attention when we come to the literature of imperialism properly so called. For the moment we simply conclude our brief sketch of economic development during the period under review with some observations on the Industrial Revolution and its varying impact on the competing powers of Western Europe and North America.

A fairly simple division, which imposes itself from the historical viewpoint, is that between the original "revolution of coal and iron" that took place between 1750 and 1850, and the subsequent age of steel, chemicals, and electricity.[13] Technology is not the whole of economics, but it is not irrelevant that those countries which forged ahead industrially during the second half of our period were better equipped than Britain to make use of the newer processes. The political unification of Germany in 1871 was made possible by military victories over Austria and France which owed something, though not everything, to the efficiency of the Prussian arms industry, symbolized by the Krupp steelworks at Essen in the Ruhr. The subsequent expansion of German steel and chemical production once more reflected an advanced technology, which in turn was helped along by an educational system that provided a fairly broad stratum of technically skilled workers and managers, and a number of outstanding scientists. Similar considerations hold for the spectacular expansion of industry and railway-building in France during the reign of Napoleon III (1852–70), and inversely for the slowdown of French industrial development after the loss of the Lorraine iron mines in 1871. For Britain, as noted above, the age of missed opportunities set in between 1880 and 1914, when stagnation at home was veiled by spectacular colonial acquisitions and a vast flow of investment capital to overseas areas—not all of them belonging to the Empire, but for the most part linked economically to Britain by the mechanism of exchange already mentioned earlier. The system was heavily weighted in favor of overseas trade and the "invisible" services provided by the City of London, all at the expense of industry and technology, which fell behind North American and German competitors. No simple explanation of this process is available. One cannot, for example, maintain that the German class structure was intrinsically favorable to technological modernization, although it is certainly the

case that Britain's social atmosphere was no help in competing
with the United States. One need only consider the case of
Japan—a highly successful newcomer with a socio-political structure even more retrograde than that of Prussia—to realize that
all such simple cause-and-effect explanations are invalid. There
may have been something in the process of German and Japanese
"nation-building" during this period which stimulated industrial
enterprise, but once we are launched upon imponderables such
as "national morale," we may as well admit that they represent
variables not reducible to causal explanation.

What is undeniable is the retrogressive effect American, German, and Japanese competition had on Britain from the 1880's
onward, when the whole liberal system underwent its first serious
crisis. The system rested upon the presupposition that a global
economy—centered upon Britain and secured by British control
of the seas—offered all countries, developed and undeveloped
alike, an optimal chance for exploiting their domestic resources
and their foreign trade opportunities. The world economy was
policed by the British navy and serviced by British capital exports. In both respects Britain acted as the guarantor of a system
from which the industrially advanced countries profited: the
United States above all, since its informal alliance with Britain
after the Civil War saved it the trouble of building up a vast
maritime establishment. When the system began to break down,
because Britain's competitors were unwilling to play the game
according to the rules of free-trade logic, "imperialism" returned.
Actually it had never disappeared, but now the veil was cast off.
Economic preponderance was gone, and mercantilist modes of
thought came back into fashion:

> In India, the formal Empire never ceased to be vital to the
> British economy. Elsewhere it appeared to become increasingly
> vital after the 1870's, when foreign competition became acute,
> and Britain sought to escape from it—and largely did escape
> from it—by a flight into her dependencies. From the 1880's "im-
> perialism"—the division of the world into formal colonies and

"spheres of influence" of the great powers . . . became universally popular among the large powers. For Britain this was a step back. She exchanged the informal empire over most of the underdeveloped world for the formal empire of a quarter of it, plus the older satellite economies.[14]

The contrast with Britain's position at the peak of the earlier era is very marked. "After the repeal of the Corn Laws, English ports were opened to the products of the whole world. Apparently, not far short of one-third of the exports of the rest of the world found their way into the United Kingdom in the 1850's and 1860's. . . . Little of this came from the empire, less than a quarter in fact. Our largest single trading-partner was the United States, accounting for nearly a quarter of all imports and of all exports. Another quarter was accounted for by the countries of Europe, which were beginning, like the U.S.A., to industrialize themselves with British equipment and ideas."[15] The Empire, other than India, did not give much direct advantage to British exports. What it did was to supply cheap food and raw materials, mostly from lands of European settlement which were either self-governing or in the process of becoming so. The acquisition of African colonies after 1880 was a poor bargain when measured against the advantage of free trade in foodstuffs and industrial goods with Europe, Canada, Argentina, and the United States. "The advantage of the strategic lines of the empire was the preservation of a world of free trade."[16] That world endured until 1914 and then collapsed in the two global wars unchained by Germany's challenge to Britain's position. The purely Continental European factors entering into this reckoning were extraneous to the Anglo-German contest. In particular, the triangular conflict among Germany, Austria-Hungary, and Czarist Russia could have been fought out on land without involving Britain, even though it did involve France (because of the Franco-Russian alliance of the 1890's). What turned these European rivalries into a global conflagration was the Anglo-German antagonism, later supplemented by

Japan's challenge to Britain and the United States. And this antagonism had its source in the weakening of Britain's over-all position toward the end of the century.

At this point, the notion of "capitalist imperialism" can at last be discriminated from the conventional employment of the term "empire" that denotes overland or overseas expansion. This is not to say that such a use of the term is illegitimate: merely that one must decide what one is talking about. There grew up in the nineteenth century a British Empire in India, a Russian Empire in Central Asia, and a French Empire in Africa. These empires were not obliged to clash, and in fact never did. Their owners were satisfied with the status quo and only asked to be left in peace, so that they might digest their conquests. The trouble was started by newcomers who did *not* possess an empire: Germany and Japan. Once this has been grasped, we can stop arguing over the meaning of "empire." Imperialist powers are not by definition obliged to own large tracts of land inhabited by conquered peoples. It is quite enough for our purpose if they are animated by a political will to bring about a forcible rearrangement of the global system controlled by their rivals.

The dual meaning of "imperialism" will be discussed in our next section, for one cannot understand the imperialist mentality without taking account of its roots in nationalism. Here we conclude with a few facts and figures culled at random from our sources. Down to the eve of 1914, the British-controlled system endured because "invisible" income from previously invested capital had come to fill the gap in Britain's payments balance. "As her industry sagged, her finance triumphed, her services as shipper, trader, and intermediary in the world's system of payments, became more indispensable. Indeed if London ever was the real economic hub of the world, the pound sterling its foundation, it was between 1870 and 1913."[17]

In 1913, Britain owned about £4,000 million worth of capital invested abroad, against a total of some £5,500 million owned by the United States, Germany, France, Belgium, and Holland put together. In financial terms, Britain was still the leading economic power; nor had her maritime empire been seriously challenged. "In the later 1850's British ships had carried about 30 per cent of the cargoes entering French or U.S. ports: by 1900 they carried 45 per cent of the French, 55 per cent of the American ones. Paradoxically the very process which weakened British production—the rise of new industrial powers, the enfeeblement of the British competitive power—reinforced the triumph of finance and trade."[18]

The 1914–18 war upset these arrangements, and the war of 1939–45 completed the wreckage. When these two epic contests were over, Britain had ceased to be the world's leading creditor nation and, indeed, had run up sizable debts to her former colonies—India above all. Capital invested abroad continued to yield a growing return, but this form of income no longer sufficed to cover the historic deficit resulting from the export balance. The payments gap now had to be filled by stepping up commodity exports to industrially developed countries, and this in turn imposed drastic rationalization measures at home. All these economic consequences flowed from the catastrophe let loose by the two world wars, and these wars in turn were precipitated by political rivalries not reducible to simple profit-and-loss calculation. The German onslaught—and later the Japanese attack—on the world system of which Britain was the guarantor had its root in the transformation German and Japanese nationalism underwent as these countries completed their industrialization and thus their adaptation to the modern world. On ordinary commonsense assumptions they would have done better to maximize their welfare in other ways, but utilitarianism had no place in their calculations. Or if it had, they did their sums wrong, for in the event none profited save the United States and Russia (soon to be challenged by China). To treat this outcome as mysterious is to ignore the simple circumstance that the British Empire perished in much the same fashion as those older empires on whose ruins it had come into being.

Notes

1. C. R. Fay, *English Economic History* (Cambridge: Heffer, 1940), p. 3.
2. Cited in Charles Wilson, *Mercantilism* (London: Routledge, 1958), p. 6. For the Historical School, see J. A. Schumpeter, *History of Economic Analysis* (London: Allen & Unwin; New York: Oxford University Press, 1954), pp. 504 ff., 808 ff.
3. Wilson, *Mercantilism*, p. 6.
4. *Ibid.*, p. 7.
5. Fay, *English Economic History*, p. 12.
6. John Maynard Keynes, *General Theory* (London: Macmillan, 1947; New York: Harcourt, Brace, 1936), p. 340.
7. Wilson, *Mercantilism*, p. 9.
8. Gustav Schmoller, *Gesammelte Aufsätze*, pp. 20 ff.; cited by Fritz Fischer, *Germany's Aims in the First World War* (New York: Norton, 1967), p. 9. Professor Fischer needs no introduction. His eminence in his chosen field is such that even his German academic colleagues have reluctantly abandoned the attempt to revert to their traditional silence on the topic of German war aims.
9. Cited in Dieter Groh, *Russland und das Selbstverständnis Europas* (Neuwied: Luchterhand, 1961), p. 264.
10. Fay, *English Economic History*, p. 10.
11. E. J. Hobsbawm, *Industry and Empire* (London: Weidenfeld & Nicolson; New York: Pantheon, 1968), p. 110.
12. E. J. Hobsbawm, *Labouring Men: Studies in the History of Labour* (London: Weidenfeld & Nicolson, 1964; Garden City: Doubleday, 1965), pp. 179 ff.; Henry Pelling, *The Origins of the Labour Party 1880–1900*, rev. ed. (Oxford: Clarendon Press; New York: Oxford University Press, 1965), *passim*.
13. W. O. Henderson, *The Industrialization of Europe 1780–1914* (London: Thames & Hudson; New York: Harcourt, Brace & World, 1969), *passim*.
14. Hobsbawm, *Industry and Empire*, pp. 123–24.
15. Michael Barratt Brown, *After Imperialism* (London: Heinemann, 1963; New York: Hillary House, 1963), p. 63.
16. *Ibid.*, p. 65.
17. Hobsbawm, *Industry and Empire*, p. 125.
18. *Ibid.*, pp. 125–26.

CHAPTER 6

Imperialism and Nationalism

THE IMPERIALIST MOVEMENT IN LATE NINETEENTH-CEN-tury and early twentieth-century Europe and America is too complex a phenomenon to lend itself to summary treatment. Yet something needs to be said about its role in promoting the era of global conflagrations after 1914. The collapse of the British-centered world economic system—the theme of the preceding chapter—cannot be treated in isolation from the growth of political currents adverse to liberalism and free trade. For Britain itself this is obvious, which is why every historian dealing with the period has found it necessary to take account of the liberal-imperialist ideology worked out by British writers between 1880 and 1914. Before turning to this topic, however, something must be said about a more general matter which is frequently neglected: the relationship of imperialism as a popular movement to the theory and practice of nationalism.

The difficulty here is that the historian is swamped by a mass of factual material impossible to summarize. Yet a simple generalization can safely be risked: imperialism as a movement—or, if one prefers, as an ideology—latched on to nationalism because no other popular base was available. But this statement can also be turned around: nationalism transformed itself into im-

81

perialism wherever the opportunity offered. It can be argued that popular patriotism was systematically corrupted when it passed into the service of the imperialist movement, but the speed with which the transformation was accomplished suggests that no deep resistance had to be overcome—not even in France, where the Revolution had given birth to a democratic and universalist faith in the essential unity of mankind. Paradoxically, it was that very universalism which became the ideological instrument of expansionist policies—"ideological" in the sense that their sponsors were taken in by their own rhetoric. Cynicism crept in at a later date, when the prophets of empire no longer took their public professions quite seriously. It was this sort of mentality that radical and socialist critics had in mind when, from the 1880's onward, they systematically denounced the colonizing enterprises of the Third Republic in Africa and Asia. Since the Republic had come into being in 1870 on the ruins of the Second Empire, it was natural to affirm that no true republican could have any dealings with "imperialism"—meaning Bonapartism. This shows how easy it is to mistake the shadow for the substance. The Orleanist liberals who took over in 1870, and the bourgeois republicans who succeeded them a decade later, had no need to invoke the spirit of Napoleon I, let alone the lamentable caricature represented by his successor. It was quite enough to maintain that French civilization was being brought to darkest Africa, just as their British contemporaries spoke of bringing Christianity to the heathen. What is more, these writers and orators were perfectly sincere, even though they neglected to add that the civilizing process was merely a by-product of something less refined. People who imagine that modern imperialism, like mercantilism before it, was merely a conspiracy got up in secret to enrich a few monopolists, will never understand how a doctrinaire radical like Clemenceau, who in the 1880's had opposed the conquest of Indochina, came two decades later to preside over the annexation of Morocco. If imperialism had lacked a popular following, this kind of behavior would be quite incomprehensible. The simple fact is that democratic politicians like Clemenceau and Lloyd George turned imperialist because that was what the voters expected of them.[1]

The voters, of course, were influenced by what they read in the newspapers, and the press was generally the vehicle of middle-class opinion. This is the justification for treating imperialist propaganda as an aspect of late-bourgeois civilization. So far as it goes, the estimate is sound. The trouble is that it fails to explain totally why liberalism went out of fashion among European politicians and newspaper owners after 1880, to be succeeded by a concentrated barrage of propaganda in favor of tariff barriers, colonial annexation, arms expenditure, and war preparation against real or presumptive rivals. These, after all, were traditional conservative remedies. The question is why they became popular in the 1880's and were eventually adopted, with some reluctance, by most liberals from about 1900 onward.

There is no problem about Tory attitudes toward India: at least since the great Indian Army mutiny of 1857, everyone knew that this huge country could be held down only by force. Moreover, Indian self-government was generally regarded as impractical even by liberals, on the grounds that several millennia of Oriental despotism had created a culture to which Western standards did not apply. If there was a division of opinion, it related to a fairly distant future. The optimists held that British rule coupled with economic development would eventually create an Indian middle class, thus making a form of parliamentary government possible; the pessimists were convinced that East and West would never meet, and that India would have to be governed imperially forever. This kind of pessimism was an ingredient of imperialist sentiment during the period under review. It fitted neatly with Tory paternalism and distrust of foreigners. It also provided American democrats with an easy target: the British were unrepentant imperialists—the proof was that they were holding India by force alone. The fact that, from an economic standpoint, India represented an anomaly within the global system of liberal imperialism was conveniently over-looked. Had it been faced, these American critics of the British Empire would have had their noses rubbed in the growing body of evidence that an American Empire was silently coming into existence.

Whether anomalous or not, British rule in India became the paradigm of Western imperialism in Asia. So did the racial animosity it created. The explorer Richard Burton had already noted Indian popular hatred of the British before the mutiny of 1857. That rising was led by local feudatories and thus had a retrogressive character, a circumstance which helps to account for its failure—the more so since the age-old Hindu-Moslem split enabled the British to use the Sikh community of the newly conquered Punjab to preserve imperial dominion. These fierce warriors took great pleasure in massacring their traditional Moslem enemies, just as they were to do in 1947, when the sub-continent was divided into the two independent states of India and Pakistan. In 1857, atrocities against British civilians—inevitable in a rising led by feudal rulers and religious fanatics—provided an excuse for savage reprisals and silenced liberal protests at home. They also gave rise to a "damned nigger" mentality among British officers and soldiers. Writing from London for *The New York Daily Tribune,* Marx cited a few typical utterances on the part of British officers; for example, "We hold court-martials on horseback, and every nigger we meet with we either string up or shoot."[2] He also introduced a line of reasoning which enabled him to place the atrocities perpetrated by Indians against English civilians in a wider historical context:

> Cruelty, like every other thing, has its fashion, changing according to time and place. Caesar, the accomplished scholar, candidly narrates how he ordered many thousand Gallic warriors to have their right hands cut off. Napoleon would have been ashamed to do this. He preferred dispatching his own French regiments, suspected of republicanism, to Santo Domingo, there to have their right hands cut off. Napoleon would have been

The last line on page 84 is incorrect. It should read: "to die of the blacks and the plague. The infamous mutilations".

committed by the Sepoys remind one of the practices of the Christian Byzantine Empire, or the prescriptions of Emperor Charles V's criminal law.[3]

Sound Hegelian reasoning this. Marx had no use for Oriental despotism and cruelty; he merely wished to deflate British self-righteousness. The Europeans, he implied, were no better than their subjects, and for the rest there was an historical explanation for the more appalling acts committed by the rebellious Sepoys: "With Hindus, whom their religion has made virtuosi in the art of self-torturing, these tortures inflicted on the enemies of their race and creed appear quite natural." Marx rarely missed a chance to vent his Lucretian distaste for religion, but his mode of reasoning was too complex for the simpler minds among his followers. In a later age they were to excuse every kind of bestiality committed against colonizers on the grounds first, that these stories were not true (they were just imperialist propaganda) and, second, that the imperialists had asked for it. But we must not judge either Darwin or Marx by their disciples. It was not Darwin's fault that the extermination of "lower races" became part of the imperialist creed, the excuse being that on Social Darwinist principles their disappearance from the face of the earth proved their unfitness to inhabit its fairer portions. Similarly, the inverted racism of Third World propaganda against whites—allegedly imperialists by nature—proves nothing against Marx or Mill, who, from their different standpoints, condemned atrocities perpetrated in the name of "civilization." The nineteenth century was a more rational and optimistic age than ours. Its representative thinkers were united by the common bond of an as yet unchallenged faith in the power of reason to improve men's behavior. The glorification of murder, beginning with the early fascists and culminating in the abominations of Hitler and other despots, belongs to a later epoch.

It is likewise remarkable that the spiritual corruption wreaked by imperialist literature was to have the most disastrous effect upon those who, though *not* lording it over subject races, yearned to do so. The actual possession of overland or overseas empires took some of the steam out of Russian, French, or British pretensions to represent the master race. Colonial armies acquired a bad reputation at home, where they were generally regarded as the last refuge of scoundrels. At the other end of the scale, the poets of empire had to pay their respects to the enemy if there was to be any glory in the imperial business. At the very least, the ferocious enemies they were fighting must be allowed a few martial virtues, or there would be nothing to celebrate. This theme runs through the popular literature of the pre-1914 age, along with a suitably stoical admiration for the legions who were defending the outposts of empire. Kipling's jingles (one can hardly describe his verse as poetry) reflect the spirit in which the British officers of the Indian Army in the 1890's—the youthful Winston Churchill among them—viewed their role in subduing savage tribesmen along the unsettled northwestern frontier of India:

> When you're wounded, and left on Afghanistan's plains,
> And· the women come out to cut up what remains,
> Just roll to your rifle, and blow out your brains.
> And go to your God like a soldier.

Hardly a Christian utterance, but suited to the mentality of Tory gentlemen in charge of a professional army. Some of these men were later to do their duty in the 1939–45 war—in the same fatalistic spirit in which they had earlier been fighting the "natives."

From the sociologist's viewpoint these were preliberal attitudes which had survived into the bourgeois age because bourgeois society, for all its pacific talk, stood in need of armed force to defend itself: if not against the proletariat at home—by the later Victorian age this was no longer a serious preoccupation—then against conquered peoples abroad. Militarism—and along with it the more primitive, aggressive, and warlike impulses—had been expelled to the frontiers of European-American civilization, there to mount guard against external foes. The duality of militarism-pacifism reproduced itself in the party game dividing conservatives from liberals: the former appealing to archaic modes of thought traditionally dominant among the landed gentry and the rural population generally; the latter reflecting the relatively peaceful outlook of middle-class burghers and industrial workers alike. These urban citizens could be galvanized into patriotic fervor by politicians and newspapers, but their ferocity was mostly verbal: they preferred to leave the actual fighting to others. Hence the typically Anglo-American compromise whereby, down to 1914–18, the dirty work was left to professionals. Conscription was regarded with disfavor. It smacked of Continental European absolutism: those military monarchies —Russia, Prussia, Austria—whose armies carried undue weight politically. But the revival of conscription in the France of the Third Republic—after Napoleon III had suffered shipwreck with his professional army in 1870—ought to have served as a warning against taking the professions of bourgeois pacifism literally. There was no neat division separating the old empires from the new republics. Democracy was not merely patriotic in its origins: it could become imperialistic too. The French made this discovery after 1870, the Americans somewhat later. Both took pains to hide the truth from themselves.

The case of France is of special interest in our context because, after 1871, the French Republic stood almost alone in a monarchical Europe. The military defeat of 1870 was in part due to reliance upon professional soldiers trained in endless colonial fighting. Whereas Prussia had universal military service, the government of Napoleon III relied upon a standing army eked out by what was known as the "blood tax." To cite a well-known historian: "All Frenchmen might be called on to serve—if France insisted on using all the healthy men who came of military age each year. But she did not, and so most of the annual 'contingent' was exempted. By means of a lottery, the necessary number of recruits, nominally 100,000, was chosen from the total of the annual 'class,' and those who drew 'bad numbers' had to serve, unless they found someone to take their place. This meant in effect that poor men with bad numbers served; richer men bought substitutes."[4] After 1871, the Republic did away with this iniquitous system—especially when the Radical Republicans got control in the 1880's, and universal service was introduced, with no exceptions allowed for the propertied classes. This was sound democratic practice. It was also a foretaste of 1914–18, when millions of men were enrolled to die in the trenches. Meantime, a colonial army—part Foreign Legion, part native levies officered by Frenchmen—remained in being along with the conscript force stationed in the motherland. The officers of course were professionals. Drawn largely from the traditionally royalist landed gentry which despised the Republic, they gave their loyalty to France's growing empire in Africa and Asia. Thus was imperialism reborn—on a solid republican-democratic foundation. The only people who thought this odd were the Socialists and after 1914 they came to terms with the system, much as the Communists did in 1945.

Imperialist thinking transcended nationalism, inasmuch as the more farsighted theorists and practitioners of the new creed realized that the nation-state was on the way out: it was too small to contain the forces let loose by the Industrial Revolution. To this esoteric wisdom, then still confined to general staffs and German professors brought up on Hegel and Clausewitz, conservative statesmen and thinkers added another subversive notion: democratic government was likewise doomed, for a democracy could not govern an empire. This was sound classical doctrine, certified by the great Roman historians on whom the ruling elites of Europe and America had been brought up. It was not contradicted by Anglo-American experience, for the British parliamentary system was oligarchic, and the American Republic did not (as yet) have an empire to administer. The seeming exception to the rule was France, for the French colonial empire expanded rapidly after the French Empire of Napoleon

III had made way for the Republic. But the Republic was bourgeois, proclaimed by middle-class lawyers in September, 1870 and saved from the proletariat (in May, 1871) when the army slaughtered the Parisian Communards. From this circumstance most Socialists derived the comforting doctrine that colonial imperialism was inherently classbound, an aspect of capitalist expansion and not likely to survive the coming of true republican democracy, with socialists in control. This amiable illusion, like many others, did not outlive the shock of 1914. Meantime most Frenchmen, but especially Frenchmen of the Left, drew moral sustenance from the fact that their country had resurrected the famous symbols of 1792, when the Convention challenged the kings of Europe. So delighted were they with their new Republic that many of them did not mind when in the 1890's France became the ally of Czarist Russia: a necessary counterweight (it was explained) to the growing might and menace of imperial Germany.

The Germans faced a different problem. Bismarck's *Reich* was an empire by definition, but confined to Central Europe: specifically, to the territory of the ancient Holy Roman Empire. Pan-Germanism—the strongest emotional force within the middle class from the 1890's onward—centered upon racial affiliations which pointed obscurely to a coming showdown with the Slavs in general and Russia in particular. On the other hand, competition with Britain led to the acquisition of colonies in Africa and ultimately to a naval race which ruined whatever chance there was of coming to terms with the British Government over Germany's claim to hegemony in Continental Europe. A more rational policy would have postponed the Anglo-German conflict in the interest of getting British support against the Franco-Russian combination. But Anglophiles who advocated such a course encountered a formidable argument: without a navy, Germany would be dependent on British goodwill and thus hampered in the pursuit of her ambitions in the Balkans and the Middle East. For the prime goal of German foreign policy during the Wilhelminian era after 1890 was not Africa but Central Europe and, more distantly, Turkey. The African colonies were merely counters in a diplomatic game. Turkey, on the other hand, represented an enormous prize. The decrepit Ottoman Empire straddled southeastern Europe and the Middle East with its growing oil resources. Control of Turkey, in addition to Austria-Hungary, would give Germany the kind of territorial and economic base to which naval strategists like Tirpitz, and economic historians like Schmoller looked forward when they envisaged the coming age of continental rivalries. The handful of African colonies could be lost without altering the balance of power. The Ottoman Empire was another matter. If Germany got control of it, there was an end to Pan-Slav hopes of Russia acquiring Constantinople. But there was also an end to British control of the East. Thus Germany's bid for empire united Russia and Britain against her.[5]

None of this poses any particular theoretical problem, whatever it may have contributed to the headaches suffered by diplomatists and general staffs. What does at first sight look odd is the ease with which nationalism could be transmuted into imperialism: not as a conspiratorial scheme pursued by governments and their advisers, but as a popular movement. For as to its popularity there is really no doubt at all: it could even draw upon working-class support, thus giving rise to the phenomenon later described by its Marxist critics as "social imperialism." The explanation clearly has to do with the familiar time lag in the assimilation of new concepts. The two most powerful political movements in the nineteenth century were nationalism and democracy, both descended from the French Revolution and thus associated with the political Left until they were harnessed by the Right. This changeover was rendered possible by the circumstance that both parties appealed to the peasantry and the lower-middle class. These strata could move in either direction. If in France the Left was generally able to drape itself in Jacobin colors, thereby associating the sentiment of patriotism with the symbols of the Republic, the Right could appeal to "eternal France." German and Russian conservatives likewise fell back on patriotic slogans, already crystallized in the doctrines of Pan-Germanism and Pan-Slavism before they became political catchwords. In each case, the popular consciousness absorbed national sentiments which were then converted into imperialist aims by the governing classes. The transition from patriotism to nationalism, let alone imperialism, was not perceived by peasants, who traditionally thought in terms of defending "the home land": a simple mental construct derived from the ordinary man's loyalty to his village or plot of land. Nationalism, unlike peasant patriotism, was an urban doctrine, the creation of schoolmasters and journalists who preached it to the middle class. Imperialism was the esoteric faith of the governing elite. These doctrines fused among intellectuals and among the army officers who staffed the various "pan" movements. The masses hardly noticed the transformation until its consequences were brought home to them by the 1914–18 war.[6]

If imperialism was not at first distinguished from ordinary nationalism, neither did anti-imperialism concern itself at the outset with anything in the economic sphere. An unimpeachable witness to the truth of this statement is Friedrich Engels who, from the 1850's until his death in 1895, devoted much of his energy to the struggle against Pan-Slavism. Any reader of his articles on this topic must be struck by his indifference to all but strictly national and racial considerations. Take the following typical passage from an article written for a liberal-democratic German journal in 1855, at a time when the Crimean war had inflamed the ancient democratic fear of Russia and its expansionist tendencies:

> The Slavic race, long divided by internal rivalries, driven back towards the East by the Germans, subjugated in part by Germans, Turks, and Hungarians, quietly reassembling its branches after 1815 through the gradual rise of Pan-Slavism, now for the first time affirms its unity and in so doing proclaims war to the

death to the Romano-Celtic and Germanic races hitherto pre-
ponderant in Europe. Pan-Slavism is not simply a movement for
national independence. It is a movement which seeks to undo
what has been created by a thousand years of history; which
cannot realize itself without wiping Turkey, Hungary, and half
of Germany from the map of Europe; and which having attained
this aim, cannot assure its permanence otherwise than through
the subjugation of Europe. From being a spiritual credo, Pan-
Slavism has transmuted itself into a political program, with
800,000 bayonets at its disposal. It leaves Europe with only one
alternative: subjugation by the Slavs or permanent destruction
of the center of their offensive strength—Russia.[7]

Substitute "China" for "Russia," and "Chinese chauvinism"
for "Pan-Slavism," and you have the theme song of a thousand
speeches and newspaper articles in the Soviet Union for the
past few years. Engels did not trouble to search for economic
causes of Slav aggression; neither do his pupils in Moscow. They
know, as he did, that nationalism is a force in its own right.

In the case of Russia and Germany alike, the transition from
patriotism to nationalism was effected in the ideological sphere
long before governments and general staffs had adopted the new
ideology. So far from being state-sponsored, these movements
were demagogic and subversive before becoming conservative and
respectable. *Volkstum* and *narodnost* were radical slogans which
terrified the autocratic rulers in Vienna, Berlin, and St. Petersburg, both before and after 1848. In the end, the governments
reluctantly came to terms with them, and the more conservative
nationalists in turn abandoned their radicalism. The classic case
is Dostoyevsky, a one-time rebel reconciled to the Orthodox
faith and transformed into a conservative upholder of the autocracy. But Pan-Slavism also retained its revolutionary wing,
typified by Bakunin who in 1873 composed an entire book on the
theme that only a popular revolution could regenerate Russia
and render it capable of confronting the newly created German
Reich. Not to mention the Yellow Peril, for Bakunin was convinced that the Chinese would one day drive across the Urals

and down to the Volga. Population pressure alone made it inevitable, and unfortunately the Czarist government was quite incompetent to deal with this very grave menace. Thus Bakunin in 1873. One can see why the authorities in St. Petersburg did not think highly of his advice. One can also see why those who were familiar with his Pan-Slav agitation thought they detected a certain lack of consistency in his anarchist utterances.[8]

British, German, Austro-Hungarian, Russian, and Ottoman policies in the three decades before 1914 centered upon what was vaguely known as "the Oriental question": a catch-phrase invented to describe the dissolution of the Turkish Empire and the maneuvering of the great powers around this increasingly dangerous piece of territory. There had already been one military contest over Turkey (the Crimean War), and another confrontation between Britain and Russia was very narrowly averted in 1878 when the British seemed ready to draw the sword on Turkey's behalf. Peace was preserved on that occasion, with Bismarck casting himself in the role of honest broker; in actual fact he sided with Britain, a circumstance not overlooked in St. Petersburg. Had his successors stuck to this line, an Anglo-German alliance might have come into being. Instead, they rashly decided to challenge France, Britain, and Russia all at once and for good measure in 1917 they took on the United States as well. This was rather too much for Germany to cope with, and military defeat resulted in 1918, with consequences that worked themselves out in 1939–45. In essentials, both wars were fought to decide whether or not Germany was to become the hegemonial power in Central, Eastern, and Southeastern Europe. This was generally recognized and in itself raises no problem: Louis XIV or Napoleon would have understood every move in the game. The new phenomenon was the infusion of popular nationalism in the shape of the various "pan" movements which mediated the transition from one age to another. These movements were populist and at times even managed to give themselves a revolutionary coloration—a circumstance very disturbing to the ruling elites until they discovered that nationalism could be harnessed to the support of traditional institutions. This is just what makes "imperialism" such a chameleon: the term changed its meaning with the passage from the age of the old absolute monarchies (all officially styled "empire") to the new world of the nation-state, and then to the specifically modern era in which nationalism was sacrificed to the real or fancied needs of supranational entities adapted to global changes in the technological sphere.

Bakunin's reflections on the topic are worth citing at some length, not only because they are intrinsically interesting, but also because they had an enormous impact upon the nascent revolutionary populist movement in Russia—a movement that was patriotic as well as socialist, and whose ideologists reserved for the Slav peoples the leading role within the coming world revolution. With the evident exhaustion of Marxism-Leninism in its official form, one may expect populist currents to regain their former prominence in the Soviet Union, especially since the Sino-Soviet conflict renders increasingly questionable the image of a global socialist "camp" organized around the U.S.S.R. Populism makes no such demands upon the imagination, being well integrated with the national Russian tradition and acceptable to patriots of all classes. It also carries unflattering implications for the Western labor movement—a movement the Soviet Union can no longer hope to control. For Bakunin had two strings to his bow: a grand vision of the coming racial conflict between the Germans and the Slavs—amply confirmed by the two European wars of our century; and a firm belief that the socialist revolution was unlikely to come first in Germany, or in any developed industrial country, for only the truly poor and destitute (the "wretched of the earth" in later parlance) could be trusted to possess the revolutionary faith. One must read Bakunin if one wants to understand the passion Lenin put into his indictment of the corrupt labor aristocracy (a doctrine, incidentally, which neither Rosa Luxemburg, nor Trotsky, Bukharin,

Gramsci, or any other important Marxist writer of the time thought worth mentioning, let alone confuting). Lenin did not cite Bakunin, but he was in some respects his heir nonetheless. Consider the following passage from Bakunin's *Gossudarstvennost i Anarkhia (Statehood and Anarchy)*, published in 1873:

> In Italy as in Russia there are a considerable number of such people [who have left the bourgeois world] .. . . But what is infinitely more important is the existence in Italy of a vast proletariat, gifted with extraordinary intelligence, but in large part illiterate and profoundly miserable, composed of 2 or 3 million urban factory workers, as well as small artisans and some 20 million peasants who possess nothing at all. . . . Nowhere perhaps is the social revolution closer than in Italy, not even in Spain. . . . There is not in Italy, as in many other European countries, a separate layer of workers in part already privileged by their high salaries, proud of a certain literary knowledge and . . . distinguished from the bourgeois only by their condition, not by their tendencies. It is above all in Germany and Switzerland that there are many workers of this kind, whereas in Italy there are very few of them. . . . What predominates in Italy is that *lumpenproletariat* of which Marx and Engels, and with them the entire German socialist-democratic school, speak with such profound and unmerited contempt; for it is only within this proletariat, and not within the bourgeoisified layer of the working masses, that there resides in totality the spirit and the force of the future social revolution.[9]

Bakunin did not require a theory of imperialist super-profits to explain why the German workers, unlike the Italians, were nonrevolutionary in temper: by his standards, they were already past hope in 1873. Engels for his part told Vera Zasulich in 1885 that in his view "the Russians are approaching their 1789."[10] This was a perfectly sound and reasonable conjecture, grounded in sociological considerations, not on crude nonsense about the rebellious temper of the *lumpenproletariat*. Engels based his forecast on his analysis of Russia as a society whose internal contradictions and strains were "held in check by an unexampled despotism, a despotism which is becoming more and more unbearable to a youth in whom the dignity and intelligence of the nation are united—there, when 1789 has once been launched, 1793 will not be long in following." No nonsense about the leading role of the working class: Engels knew perfectly well that in a backward country such as Russia the fight against absolutism came first, and that the decisive push would come from the radical intelligentsia. On this point at least, the more sensible populists and the Marxists were in agreement.

If one now turns to Bakunin's apocalyptic vision of a coming showdown between Russia and China, one finds that the old Slavophile had simply transferred his attention from Russia's western frontier to its Siberian possessions. *Gossudarstvennost i Anarkhia* is largely devoted to the German-Slav antagonism, the German threat to Russia's preponderance in the Baltic, the historic Russian longing for Constantinople, the follies of Czarist diplomacy, and other topical concerns. By contrast, the Chinese menace is dealt with briefly, but what Bakunin has to say about it is still worth reading after almost a century:

> China alone counts 400 million, or according to others 600 million inhabitants, who are evidently cramped within the frontiers of the Celestial Empire and in ever growing numbers transplant themselves in an irresistible current, some to Australia, others across the Pacific to California; other masses may finally displace themselves toward the north and northeast. And what then? Then, in the twinkling of an eye, Siberia, the entire territory extending from Tartary to the Ural mountains and the Caspian Sea will cease to be Russian. . . . How is one to arrest the irruption of the Chinese masses who will not only invade the whole of Siberia, including our new possessions in Central Asia, but will also expand beyond the Urals down to the Volga!
>
> Such is the danger which menaces us all but fatally from the eastern side. One does wrong to despise the Chinese masses. They are dangerous simply by virtue of their considerable number, dangerous because their excessive proliferation renders virtually impossible their future existence within the frontiers of China. . . . Let us also note that of late they have begun to familiarize themselves with modern arms and European discipline, that

latest official fruit of our statist civilization. Just ally this disci-pline, the acquirement of new arms and modern tactics, with the primitive barbarism of the Chinese masses, with their total lack of any idea of human protest, of all instinct of liberty, with their habit of servile obedience . . . consider the monstrous enormity of the Chinese population . . . and you will understand how great is the peril which menaces us from the side of the East.[11]

The author of these lines was a better prophet than those among his Leninist pupils who after 1917 thought they had exorcized the specter by helping the Chinese revolution to attain its goals. For these goals were *national,* hence incompatible with the hegemony of a rival empire in Asia.

Notes

1. For the general topic see Heinz Gollwitzer, *Europe in the Age of Imperialism* (London: Thames & Hudson; New York: Harcourt, Brace & World, 1969), *passim;* for the literature of the period see V. G. Kiernan, *The Lords of Human Kind: European Attitudes Towards the Outside World in the Imperial Age* (London: Weidenfeld & Nicolson; Boston: Little, Brown, 1969), *passim;* for the ideology of Social Darwinism and its various offshoots, see Bernard Semmel, *Imperialism and Social Reform: English Social-Imperialist Thought 1895–1914* (London: Allen & Unwin; New York: Hillary House, 1960), *passim;* for the Fabian contribution to this murky stream see A. M. McBriar, "The Fabians, Imperialism, Tariff Reform, and War" in A. M. McBriar, *Fabian Socialism and English Politics 1884–1918* (Cambridge: Cambridge University Press, 1966; New York: Cambridge University Press, 1962), pp. 119 ff.; for an eloquent exposition of British imperialist ideology at the peak of the movement, see A. P. Thornton, *The Imperial Idea and Its Enemies: A Study in British Power* (London: Macmillan; New York: St. Martin, 1959), *passim;* for an attempt to show that the partition of the globe among rival powers after 1880 had no rational economic motivation, see J. Gallagher and R. Robinson, "The Imperialism of Free Trade," *Economic History Review,* 7, no. 1 (1953). The theme is discussed at greater length in J. A. Schumpeter's essay collection entitled *Imperialism and Social Classes,* ed. Paul M. Sweezy (Oxford: Basil Blackwell, 1951), *passim.* The standard

liberal critique of British imperialism was initiated by J. A. Hobson in *Imperialism: A Study* (1902; rev. ed., London: Allen & Unwin, 1948; Ann Arbor: University of Michigan Press, 1965), *passim*. The imperialist literature itself is virtually coterminous with conservative and ruling-class thought in the age of Theodore Roosevelt, Joseph Chamberlain, and William II. Amidst this flood, A. T. Mahan, *The Influence of Sea Power upon History 1660–1783* (New York: Sagamore Press, 1957), is a distinctly superior specimen and can also claim to have altered the current of affairs inasmuch as it became the Bible of American, British, Japanese, and German rulers, politicians, and admirals from the day of its publication in 1890 down to the outbreak of war in 1914, and perhaps down to Pearl Harbor and the Japanese-American conflict of 1941–45.

2. Article of September 4, published in the *New York Daily Tribune*, 16 September 1857; reprinted in Karl Marx and Friedrich Engels, *The First Indian War of Independence* (Moscow, 1959), p. 93; and in S. Avineri, ed., *Karl Marx on Colonialism and Modernization* (Garden City: Doubleday, 1968), p. 213. For the general effect of the 1857 bloodbath on British-Indian relations, see Kiernan, *The Lords of Human Kind*, pp. 46 ff.

3. Marx, *The First Indian War of Independence*, pp. 93–94.

4. D. W. Brogan, *The Development of Modern France (1870–1939)* (London: Hamish Hamilton, 1940; New York: Harper & Row, rev. ed., 1966), p. 16.

5. Fritz Fischer, *Germany's Aims in the First World War* (New York: Norton, 1967), pp. 9 ff., 31 ff., 46 ff., 98 ff. Once war had broken out in 1914, Germany's imperial appetite began to encompass the creation of a Central African colonial empire as well, but domination of *Mitteleuropa* always remained at the core of it. A customs union with Austria-Hungary and annexations in Russia were essential features of this program, which had already been worked out before 1914 by leading industrialists such as Walter Rathenau, subsequently one of the more prominent figures of the shortlived Weimar Republic. Expansion into the Near East followed as a matter of course.

6. Gollwitzer, *Europe in the Age of Imperialism*, pp. 42 ff. But it does not follow that imperialism was unpopular. The notion that it never had a mass following is on a par with the belief that fascism was the conscious creation of a few demagogues and never attracted anyone but ruined shopkeepers. Such beliefs, firmly held by the more simple spirits on the Left after 1919, were responsible for major political disasters during the interwar period.

7. Friedrich Engels, "Deutschland und der Panslawismus," *Neue Oder-Zeitung*, 21 April 1855; reprinted in Karl Marx and Friedrich Engels, *Werke*, vol. 11 (East Berlin, 1961), pp. 193–94; see also Engels's article in the same journal of April 24, where Austrian Pan-Slavism is distinguished from its Russian branch, and Metternich is given some credit for having perceived the Russian menace. His repressive measures failed (Engels observes) because his regime could not permit that "free development of the German and Hungarian spirit which was more than sufficient to exorcise the Slav specter."

This line of thought went back to 1848 and eventually came to rank among the treasured possessions of all but a handful of German and Austro-Hungarian Social Democrats. For obvious reasons, Leninist writers have never been eager to emphasize this embarrassing circumstance which makes nonsense of the assertion that the German and Austrian Socialists in 1914 betrayed their spiritual heritage. It would be truer to say that they remained faithful to it after it had ceased to be relevant. For Marx's views on the subject, which did not differ fundamentally from Engels's except that he was friendlier to the Poles, see the two pamphlets respectively entitled *Secret Diplomatic History of the Eighteenth Century* and *The Story of the Life of Lord Palmerston*—both originally published in British and American journals between 1853 and 1857, and now available in book form, edited by Lester Hutchinson (London: Lawrence & Wishart, 1969); also Karl Marx, *Manuskripte über die polnische Frage (1863–1864)* (The Hague: Mouton, 1961).

8. See Karl Marx, *Konspekt von Bakunins "Staatlichkeit und Anarchie,"* in *Werke,* vol. 18 (East Berlin, 1962), pp. 599 ff., esp. p. 622. Written in 1874–75, but not published at the time, Marx's critical survey of Bakunin's curious mixture of anarchism and Pan-Slavism still claims a certain topical interest.

9. Tr. from the French version, *Étatisme et Anarchie,* in *Archives Bakounine* (Leiden: E. J. Brill, 1967), p. 206. For the subsequent fortunes of this work and the post-Revolution reprints of 1919 and 1922, see the editorial Introduction. The pamphlet had a profound impact upon the Russian populists, a circumstance confirmed in 1876 by the Blanquist writer Peter Tkachev, who differed radically from Bakunin on the issue of "spontaneity" versus centralized organization. It was of course the student youth who took up these ideas and transmitted them to later generations of revolutionaries, Lenin's contemporaries among them. For the rest, one has only to peruse *State and Revolution* (1917) to realize that Lenin—while carefully citing Marx and Engels in support of his theses—had effected a fusion of the Bakuninist and the Blanquist inheritance.

10. Karl Marx and Friedrich Engels, *Selected Correspondence* (Moscow: Foreign Languages Publishing House, 1956), p. 459.

11. Bakunin, *Étatisme et Anarchie,* pp. 282–83.

CHAPTER 7

Imperialism and Revolution

WE ARE NOW OBLIGED TO MAKE A DETOUR THROUGH economic theorizing before returning to history. This procedure is imposed by the nature of the subject, but also by the fact that, after 1900, imperialism was perceived primarily as an economic relationship. The debate thus came to turn very largely on considerations having to do with the peculiar mechanism of capitalist market economics. Ever since the Russian Revolution dramatized the issue, this is what imperialism has meant to the general public, but the theoretical discussion started some twenty years prior to that event.

Before turning to this important and complex debate, it will be useful to eliminate a misconception current among people who have come to associate the topic with the conflict between the Third World and the industrial superpowers, whence the notion that capitalism—or Western capitalism plus Soviet state-socialism—relates to the "underdeveloped" world in a manner similar to the classical colonialism of the nineteenth century. In its crude form, this thesis is plainly untenable. It can be dealt with by asking a simple question: what *economic* damage has the "loss" of China done to American capitalism since 1950, or to Soviet state-socialism since 1960? Plainly, none at all. It has rather freed these two superpowers of the tiresome obligation to provide development funds for China, thus throwing an additional burden on the Chinese people. To this one may, if one is so minded, add the grisly query: what difference would it make to Western Europe and North America if the entire population of the Indian subcontinent were wiped out by famine, pestilence, or some other catastrophe? The answer presumably is that the British would then have to go without tea. What other economic consequences such an appalling human disaster would have is not easy to discover.

There exists, however, a more sophisticated form of the argument which does not make the mistake of treating India and China as urgently needed sources of raw materials and foodstuffs, or as markets for Western and Soviet exports. This approach recognizes the growing irrelevance of the Third World from the standpoint of the fully industrialized countries. It builds its projections upon the dialectic of underdevelopment, neocolonial exploitation, increasing antagonism between the rich and the poor, and consequent revolutionary movements in the impoverished lands of the Third World. This is a line of thought which has to be taken seriously, if only because in its Maoist guise it has amalgamated with nationalism to become the official creed of China. The trouble is that not infrequently it gets mixed up with arguments stressing the growing dependence of Western— notably American—industry upon imported minerals. There is no inherent contradiction in these notions, but we need to be clear just what we are talking about.

In its academic form, the thesis relies upon comparisons with the mercantilist era. During that bygone age, colonial exploitation of the tropics helped to finance Western industrialization, and the new industries in turn unloaded their surplus commodity exports of consumer goods upon colonial territories owned or controlled by Holland, England, France, and other European powers. This was the essence of what in French literature came to be known as the *pacte colonial*. What is nowadays styled "neocolonialism" represents a different relationship: contractual bargaining between advanced and backward countries whereby the former undertake to assist the industrialization of the latter, on the understanding that loans will be reimbursed and investment capital will not be confiscated. Since the loans cannot in fact be repaid with interest, and since the profits of Western corporations are for the most part funneled back to the metropolis, the relationship remains unequal, although it may look reasonable on paper. Moreover, this form of modernization proceeds too slowly to catch up with the population explosion.

Taken in the abstract, there appears to be no reason why a major industrial country—whether capitalist or socialist—should not assume the temporary burden of helping to modernize backward ("underdeveloped") areas. Likewise a backward country may lift itself by its own bootstraps. This, after all, is what occurred in the case of Japan, and Japan has become a more important market for Western industrial exports than the rest of Asia combined. It is also, however, a competitor. Japan, for historical reasons, escaped from the typical colonial relationship and has now assumed the rank of a major industrial power. As such, it provides markets for Western exports of consumer goods, whereas colonial profits are typically derived from extractive industries operating with cheap labor and producing oil or minerals to feed the industries of the advanced countries. Why then should the West—America above all—not assist other countries to follow the Japanese road? Setting aside domestic barriers to modernization, it would appear to be in the interest of all concerned to make the necessary means available. This, after all, is the only way in which the productive forces of the Third World can be developed to the point where these countries become worth-while partners in international exchange.

If the question is posed in this form, the more consistent ideologists of the Trotskyist or Maoist school (in practice the two are becoming difficult to distinguish, since the Maoists are incompetent when it comes to theory and have to fall back on arguments worked out for them by Trotskyist writers) are reduced to the assertion that capitalism, by its nature, *cannot* promote the full industrialization of its former colonies. The argument relies upon the Leninist identification of capitalism with imperialism. The latter by definition impedes the modernization of backward countries, while relying upon cheap labor to obtain raw materials for the metropolis. Hence, so the logic runs, a drive to industrialize the undeveloped areas, in the hope of extracting higher profits at a later date, while in principle meeting the requirements of economic rationality, would be self-liquidating so far as imperialism is concerned, for the developed countries—capitalist or nominally socialist—would have to sacrifice some of their profits or some of their domestic consumption for the sake of the undeveloped. On ethical grounds, this is of course what they ought to be doing, but it can also be argued that self-preservation alone is an adequate motive. After all, the widening gulf between the industrial centers and the Third World is potentially dangerous for all concerned. Nonetheless, conventional radical thinking affirms that such a self-liquidation of imperialism is not going to occur, because in the short run it is more profitable to maintain the present unequal relationship. At the same time, it is held that colonial resources are crucially important to the functioning of Western capitalism, which would be strangled without access to these raw materials.[1]

The argument suffers from trying to prove too much. If the undeveloped countries are becoming irrelevant to the highly industrialized centers, they cannot at the same time be essential to them. If they are relevant as sources of oil, bauxite, tin, chrome, nickel, manganese, and other raw materials, then they are likely to accumulate capital for their own industrialization: if necessary by expropriating foreign holdings located on their territories, but more probably by squeezing extra revenue out of them. In fact this is already happening in the oil-producing countries, and for the simplest reason: it does not pay a foreign government or corporation to quarrel with a local nationalist regime at the risk of having its installations wrecked or confiscated. Thus in general the symbiotic relationship between such regimes and the West (or the Soviet Union) does not profit *only* the stronger party.

Since the whole chain of reasoning starts from an argument developed by Lenin in 1916, we need not at this point consider the rival theory of imperialism suggested by Rosa Luxemburg in 1913, but there is a link between Lenin and the analysis of finance capital and protectionism associated with the Austro-Marxist school. The latter found a critic in J. A. Schumpeter, but his explanation of the phenomenon of imperialism embodied some suggestions that were first put forward by Rudolf Hilferding and other Marxists around 1910 and even earlier by Karl Kautsky. This debate, which climaxed during the 1914–18 war, was itself a sequel to the quarrel between conservative protectionists and liberal free-traders in Britain, and is thus closely related to the theme of the preceding chapter. On the Marxist side, it ran its course between 1910 and 1930, little being added afterward to the theoretical core of the argument then worked out by the protagonists. Liberal critics of imperialism had already found a notable champion in J. A. Hobson as early as 1902. It is worth noting here that the current American debate on the question in part reproduces this earlier British controversy, although the notion of a fundamental "North-South" division separating the industrially advanced countries—including the Soviet Union—from the backward regions of the globe is new and has introduced a political line-up that cuts across the East-West antagonism sometimes described as the cold war. It is equally worth stressing that, as a consequence of the Maoist retreat from Marxism-Leninism to populism, there has arisen the notion that the peasantry rather than the industrial proletariat is the class destined to make an end of imperialism: the latter term now applied to all the industrially advanced countries, and, within the latter, encompassing the working class along with the rest of the population. This notion represents a complete break with Marxism, a circumstance that has not prevented some of its defenders from claiming the inheritance of Marx on the grounds that revolutionaries must always side with the exploited, whether they be slaves, serfs, or peasant proprietors victimized by colonial relationships. Admirable in its resolute disregard of all but moral considerations, this doctrine seems closer in spirit to Tolstoy or Gandhi than to the founder of modern socialism.

Some familiarity with the argument set out in Lenin's *Imperialism, the Highest Stage of Capitalism* (1916) may these days be taken for granted, but it is useful to remind ourselves wherein the chief innovation lay.[2] Hobson had in 1902 described British imperialism as an outcrop of protectionist and militarist tendencies; in other words, he regarded it as a reactionary movement, a reversion to mercantilism. "The economic root of Imperialism," he wrote, "is the desire of strong organized industrial and financial interests to secure and develop at the public expense and by the public force private markets for their surplus goods and their surplus capital. War, militarism, and a 'spirited foreign policy' are the necessary means to this end."[3] Kautsky's explanation of imperialism in 1914–15 was more complex and sophisticated, as befitted a Marxist, but ran along similar lines, —a circumstance obscured by Lenin's polemics against him. Hilferding, on the other hand, although politically associated with Kautsky, was acceptable to Lenin as a writer because, in his 1910 work, he had established a connection between imperialism and "finance capital," with special reference to the great investment banks. Lenin approvingly cited his remark, "Finance capital does not want liberty, it wants domination,"[4] and then went on to develop his own thesis that imperialism represented "the monopoly stage of capitalism." This formulation differed somewhat from Hilferding's conclusion, and clashed with Kautsky's assessment, which rested on the belief that imperialist rivalry among the leading powers was merely one possibility among others: there might be less dangerous and more profitable solutions—for example, "the joint exploitation of the world by internationally united finance capital in place of the mutual rivalries of national finance capitals. Such a new phase of capitalism is at any rate conceivable." The indignàtion this suggestion evoked in Lenin's breast[5] must strike the reader as puzzling—unless he remembers that Kautsky was a pacifist, whereas Lenin was convinced that imperialism as a world system was fated to go down in a series of shattering wars and revolutions. On Kautsky's assumption—which was quite compatible with Hobson, and in part derived from him—"ultra-imperialism," as he termed it, might evolve into a stable, albeit retrogressive, system of exploitation, with imperialist rivalries reduced to a minimum. This perspective struck Lenin as both philistine and implausible: wars among the imperialist powers would continue. The reason he gives is interesting:

> The question has only to be presented clearly for any other than a negative answer to be impossible. This is because the only conceivable basis under capitalism for the division of spheres of influence, interests, colonies, etc., is a calculation of the *strength* of those participating, their general economic, financial, military strength, etc. And the strength of these participants in the division does not change to an equal degree, for the *even* development of different undertakings, trusts, branches of industry, or countries is impossible under capitalism. Half a century ago Germany was a miserable, insignificant country, if her capital strength is compared with that of the Britain of that time; Japan compared with Russia in the same way. Is it "conceivable" that in ten or twenty years' time the relative strength of the imperialist powers will have remained *unchanged?* It is out of the question.[6]

Uneven development was inherent in capitalism—especially in cartelized and trustified monopoly capitalism—and imperialist wars would result from continuous shifts in the balance of power. The conclusion, while important to Lenin, was only very loosely integrated into the general framework of his argument, which centered on the thesis that—as he put it—"in its economic essence imperialism is monopoly capitalism." This theme—developed on the basis of Hilferding's work which had traced the disappearance of free competition and laissez faire—ran alongside another strand of thought suggested by the colonial partition of the globe in the last quarter of the nineteenth century. Together, both constituted the structure of imperialism: a global system within which peaceful "re-divisions" were excluded because the various sectors of the capitalist world economy developed at different speeds, so that the balance of forces was constantly being upset. The rival imperialisms could not come to terms peacefully, not even for the purpose of jointly exploiting the rest of the globe. Lenin was writing in 1916 under the impact of the first Anglo-German war. One can only conjecture what he might have said of a world system organized around the United States, as the nineteenth-century system had been organized around Britain. Even less easy is it to imagine his comments on the triangular relationship linking the United States, the Soviet Union, and China: the two latter nominally socialist, yet to all appearances quite capable of waging a nuclear war for the sake of territory in Siberia. Still, Lenin, like everyone else, was aware that imperialism antedated capitalism:

> Colonial policy and imperialism existed before the latest stage of capitalism, and even before capitalism. Rome, founded on slavery, pursued a colonial policy and practiced imperialism. But "general" disquisitions on imperialism which ignore, or put into the background, the fundamental difference between socio-economic formations, inevitably turn into the most vapid banality or bragging, like the comparison: "Greater Rome and Greater Britain." Even the capitalist colonial policy of previous stages of capitalism is essentially different from the colonial policy of finance capital.[7]

This seems hardly conclusive as an argument against the possibility of a world imperialist cartel. Furthermore, the fact that the most varied socio-economic formations had spawned the phenomenon of imperialism might have served as a warning that the disappearance of capitalism would not necessarily bring universal peace. However, in Lenin's perspective, the global

revolt against imperialist exploitation was an aspect of the socialist revolution. That accomplished and class domination abol-
ished, what reason would the emancipated peoples have for
waging war on each other? Nationalism? But this sentiment had
historically arisen alongside bourgeois society and would give
way to the internationalism of the working class. The 1917
preface to the new edition of *Imperialism,* and even more so the
1920 preface to the French and German editions, were composed
at a time when the Russian Revolution seemed to prefigure a
global uprising. But the essential consistency of Lenin's argument does not depend upon considerations having to do with
the ups and downs of the revolutionary wave. To his mind, the
struggle for self-determination within the multinational empires
of the Habsburgs and the Romanovs was part and parcel of a
universal combat against imperialism in all its forms. The 1914–
18 war had bridged the gap between radical democracy and
proletarian socialism, for both the old dynastic and the new
capitalist empires were responsible for its outbreak. The opening
passage of an article he composed in the autumn of 1914 pulled
the strands of the argument together:

> The European war, which the governments and the bourgeois
> parties of all countries have been preparing for decades, has
> broken out. The growth of armaments, the extreme intensifica-
> tion of the struggle for markets in the latest—the imperialist—
> stage of capitalist development in the advanced countries, and the
> dynastic interests of the more backward East European mon-
> archies were inevitably bound to bring about this war, and have
> done so. Seizure of territory and subjugation of other nations, the
> ruining of competing nations and the plunder of their wealth
> . . . these comprise the sole actual content, importance, and sig-
> nificance of the present war.[8]

By 1916 Lenin was polemicizing against Kautsky, who—in an
article composed shortly before the outbreak of war and published in his journal, the *Neue Zeit,* on September 11, 1914—
had presented an interpretation of imperialism as a form of

exploitation of backward agrarian countries by the capitalist powers. Kautsky's analysis, which owed much to Hilferding and something to Luxemburg, duly made the point that protectionism had succeeded free trade. He also noted the growing pressure upon Britain, the imperialist reaction in England itself, and the growth of capital exports. All this was fully in tune with both liberal and Marxist thinking as it had developed since Hobson, as was Kautsky's stress upon the burden of militarism. Why then did Lenin take such violent objection to it? Largely because Kautsky, with his habitual optimism, had affirmed that imperialism was a retrograde phenomenon which did not really serve the interest of modern capitalism, if the system was administered rationally. Imperialism, by way of the arms race, interfered with capital accumulation and was thus a self-defeating operation. It was "digging its own grave."

> From a means to develop capitalism, it is becoming a hindrance to it. Nevertheless, capitalism need not yet be at the end of the line . . . from a purely economic standpoint it is not impossible that capitalism may go through yet another phase, the translation of cartelization into foreign policy: a phase of *ultra-imperialism* . . . whose perils lie in another direction, not that of the arms race and the threat to world peace.

This was a perfectly sensible prognosis, but Lenin would have none of it: imperialist wars would continue and they would eventually wreck the system. Thus Lenin in 1916. A few years later, in July, 1920, the preface to the French and German editions of *Imperialism* shifts the emphasis by omitting the old dynastic empires:

> It is proved in the pamphlet that the war of 1914–18 was imperialist (that is, an annexationist, predatory, war of plunder) on the part of both sides; it was a war for the division of the world, for the partition and repartition of colonies and spheres of influence of finance capital, etc.[9]

The "more backward East European monarchies" still worth mentioning in 1914 have disappeared from sight. After all, in

1920, Czarist Russia, Austria-Hungary, and the Hohenzollern monarchy were no more, and there was no need to remind the reader of their misdeeds. The argument had come to focus upon the specifically capitalist nature of modern imperialism:

> It is precisely irrefutable summarized data of this kind that I quoted in describing the *partition of the world* in 1876 and 1914 . . . and the division of the world's *railways* in 1890 and 1913. . . . Railways are a summation of the basic capitalist industries, coal, iron, and steel; a summation and the most striking index of the development of world trade and bourgeois-democratic civilization. How the railways are linked up with large-scale industry, with monopolies, syndicates, cartels, trusts, banks, and the financial oligarchy is shown in the preceding chapters of the book. The uneven distribution of the railways, their uneven development—sums up, as it were, modern monopolist capitalism on a world-wide scale. And this summary proves that imperialist wars are absolutely inevitable under *such* an economic system, *as long as* private property in the means of production exists.
>
> The building of railways seems to be a simple, natural, democratic, cultural, and civilizing enterprise. . . . But as a matter of fact the capitalist threads, which in thousands of different inter-crossings bind these enterprises with private property in the means of production in general, have converted this railway construction into an instrument for oppressing *a thousand million* people (in the colonies and semi-colonies), that is, more than half the population of the globe that inhabits the dependent countries, as well as the wage-slaves of capital in the "civilized" countries.[10]

Marx had predicted a new war between Germany and France (this time allied with Czarist Russia) from the day Bismarck demanded Alsace-Lorraine in 1870, and Engels had looked forward with trepidation to a great European war in 1890, when it became clear that Pan-Germanism and Pan-Slavism were about to collide over the decaying body of the Turkish Empire.[11] This perspective had guided the Second International since its founding in 1889, and Lenin had inherited it. But by 1920 he no longer needed it. The inevitability of war in the modern age could now be inferred from "uneven development" alone: no mention of Constantinople, or of the European power balance which underlay the pre-1914 alliances. The 1914–18 war had become essentially a conflict between Britain and Germany, and the wars of the future were going to be determined by similar rivalries.

> Capitalism has grown into a world system of colonial oppression and of the financial strangulation of the overwhelming majority of the population of the world by a handful of "advanced" countries. And this "booty" is shared between two or three powerful world plunderers armed to the teeth (America, Great Britain, Japan), who are drawing the whole world into *their* war over the division of *their* booty.[12]

The "parasitism and decay" of this imperialist capitalism expressed itself in two interconnected ways: a handful of "advanced" countries plundered the rest of the world, and they did so by way of capital exports. These investments yielded colossal profits and "out of such enormous *superprofits* . . . it is *possible to bribe* the labor leaders and the upper stratum of the labor aristocracy. And that is just what the capitalists of the 'advanced' countries are doing."[13] Too bad the "labor aristocracy" turned out to be the core of the newly formed Communist parties (as it had been the historic carrier of socialist ideas ever since the 1830's, when socialism came into being). Lenin, in 1920, had found a formula which enabled him to integrate anticolonialism within the general framework of his theorizing. He could not well foresee that half a century later these slogans would be taken up in Peking and turned against his own successors.

For by the 1970's the technological disparity between the U.S.S.R. and China had become so blatant as to raise in the minds of China's rulers the question of whether, on Leninist principles, the Soviet Union might not have to be regarded as an "imperialist" power. Support for this assessment could be found both in Lenin's earlier writings (when he was still concerned with Czarist annexations in Asia and elsewhere) and in

Imperialism, where he affirmed that the material base of imperial domination lay in uneven economic growth and in the systematic exploitation of the undeveloped countries by the more advanced ones. As for the institution of public ownership in Russia after 1917, one could get around this difficulty by asserting that private capitalism had simply been replaced by state capitalism, the *bourgeoisie* by a privileged bureaucracy. But if this had been the outcome of a proletarian revolution, then what guarantee was there that China would not suffer the same fate? At this point, Maoism discloses its essentially Rousseauist character: It replaces class analysis with social psychology. China is to be regenerated by an act of will, purified of "feudal remnants" (which it never possessed), purged of bourgeois sentiments still prevalent among nominal Communists, and in general subjected to the rule of virtue. This kind of puritanism is a feature of every major revolution. Its "proletarian" content is nil, and it is plain that its leaders have not the faintest inkling of what Marxism is about.

But although mired in primitive thought forms (nationalism above all), the Chinese are still able to make use of that element in Leninism which connects it with the Marxist critique of imperialism: the indictment of monopoly capital as the instrument of global exploitation. If it is the case that the existence of a handful of advanced countries necessarily aggravates the underdevelopment of the remainder, then the cleavage between American capitalism and Soviet "socialism" does indeed become insignificant. Which is where we came in. But before going further into this matter, there is still something to be said about Lenin's theory of imperialism and its relevance to the age that terminated in 1945.

Marxists have traditionally held that European overseas expansion since the sixteenth century was an aspect of capitalism, in the sense that it was both cause and consequence of the socioeconomic transformation originally begun by the Italian city-states and culminating in the Industrial Revolution. Mercantilist policy, as we have seen, was thoroughly imperialist and the driving force behind it was the urge to amass *national* capital in competition with rival powers. All this took shape during the pioneering age of capitalism, when production was still carried on in small competitive units. In what sense, then, can imperialism be described as the "highest stage" of capitalism, when in point of fact it made its appearance during an early transitional phase? Lenin's answer to this question differs from Hobson's in that he regards modern imperialism not as an aberration, but as the norm of capitalist development in its final monopolistic stage. If this is accepted, it follows that the system is moribund. For if monopoly capitalism entails the forcible subjugation of the world by a handful of overdeveloped imperialist countries, then the mounting hostility of the remainder must in the long run be fatal to the prospect of further development along capitalist lines. "World revolution" is now concretized in Lenin's veritable "testament"—the article published in *Pravda* on March 4, 1923, a few days before he suffered the paralyzing stroke that laid him low:

> In the last analysis, the outcome of the struggle will be determined by the fact that Russia, India, China, etc., account for the overwhelming majority of the population of the globe. And during the past few years it is this majority that has been drawn into the struggle for emancipation with extraordinary rapidity, so that in this respect there cannot be the slightest doubt what the final outcome of the world struggle will be. In this sense, the complete victory of socialism is fully and absolutely assured.[14]

In a certain fundamental sense this was to become and remain the official Soviet perspective on world affairs until Stalin's death exactly thirty years after the publication of Lenin's *Pravda* article. For whatever else he sacrificed, Stalin never made a real break with the Leninist belief in an inevitable East-West confrontation pitting Russia and Asia against the counterrevolutionary and imperialist West. This conclusion followed quite logically from Lenin's concept of imperialism, and it was this part of his thinking that—via the Stalinist heritage—eventually entered into the theory and practice of Maoism. By now of course it is no longer in accord with the political line-up, the Soviet Union having become, in Maoist terminology, an imperialist power in league with the United States.[15]

Is this simply a matter of shifting alignments due to incalculable political and personal factors, or does it point up a fault in the original theoretical construction? If the expansion of empires historically antedates the capitalist era—let alone the phase of fully developed monopolistic capitalism after 1900—then there seems to be no good reason why imperialism (in the sense of territorial conquest and the acquisition of "empty space") should not endure into the socialist age. There may be no urgent economic drive behind it, but a bureaucracy (or any other political elite in control of a major power) may feel impelled to extend its control for political and military reasons alone. In the 1930's the Stalinist regime chose to industrialize at breakneck speed (and to liquidate the peasantry as a class, while holding working-class living standards to the absolute minimum, through the institution of terrorism and forced labor) for what was primarily a political reason: the conviction that within measurable time the Soviet Union would have to confront a major military challenge. As it turned out, this forecast proved correct, though it may also have been self-fulfilling in that Stalin gave Hitler all the help he needed to come to power and thereafter provided him with an incentive for attacking the Soviet Union while there was still time to crush it. Stalin's heirs might be forgiven for thinking that this was a valuable lesson. They might also suppose that an American-Chinese alliance could prove even more menacing to Russia than the German-Japanese pact concluded in the late 1930's. Hence the desire to make sure that America's favored ally, the Kuomintang, should not obtain control of China.

So far, Stalinist strategy makes perfect sense in terms of Lenin's last writings. On the other hand, a triangular relationship pitting the Soviet Union against a hostile China governed by self-styled Communists, with the West in the role of arbiter or onlooker, cannot be accommodated within the Leninist framework of 1920. It does no good to say that this change has occurred because Lenin's heirs have defaulted, for on Lenin's assumptions such a reversal of roles is not explicable. If his analysis was correct, two events ought to have occurred after 1945: the Sino-Soviet alliance should have remained in being, and Western imperialism should have suffered a mortal blow from the loss of its colonial possessions in Africa and Asia. Alternatively, if it be said that Western capitalism survived, even though imperialism—in the form it had assumed around 1920—was wrecked by World War II and its aftermath, then it seems to follow that imperialism was after all *not* the "highest stage" of capitalism, but merely a passing political arrangement which in due course was replaced by a new sort of relationship between the rich and the poor, the developed and the undeveloped, the oppressors and the oppressed. And where does one place the Soviet Union in this picture? On the assumptions current in the literature of the ultra-Left, every developed industrial country, whether socialist or not, participates automatically in the oppression and exploitation of the Third World simply by virtue of the latter's economic lag. But if this is so, then the old distinction between socialism and imperialism is untenable. Whichever way one looks at it, Lenin's writings during the last years of his life are no longer a safe guide even for Leninists.

In its original form, Lenin's theory of imperialism had a dual function. In the first place it was intended to account for the surge of European and American overseas expansion during the last quarter of the nineteenth century and for the national conflicts resulting therefrom. Secondly, it attempted to explain structural changes within late capitalism, variously described as the age of finance capital or of monopoly. In a later version, the analysis was to encompass the phenomenon of fascism as well. For Paul Sweezy, writing in 1942, "fascism, as it exists in Germany and Italy, is one form which imperialism assumes in the age of redivision. . . . Fascism arises under certain specific historical conditions which are in turn the product of the impact of imperialist wars of redivision on the economic and social structure of advanced capitalist nations."[16] This cautious formulation is flexible enough to embrace phenomena such as Japanese militarism after 1931, which can be classified as imperialist but not as fascist since in Japan there was neither a popular mass movement nor an attempt to establish a one-party state. But just because the formula permits major deviations from the rule, it is not very helpful as an explanation of why fascism arose in such different cases as Italy, then a relatively backward country when measured by industrial standards, and Germany, an extremely advanced industrial nation. Moreover, it ignores the simultaneous growth of fascist movements in such countries as Poland, Rumania, and Hungary which could not well be credited with imperialist tendencies. Neither does it help much to be told: "The ideology and program of fascism reflect the social position of the middle classes and in this respect are merely an intensification of attitudes which have already been shown to be characteristic of imperialism."[17] Who or what are "the middle classes"? Italian and German fascism arose after 1918 among nationalist officers returning from the war, intellectuals (some of them former socialists or syndicalists) in search of a new orientation, students attracted by pseudosocialist rant against "finance capital," artistic bohemia, and the *lumpenproletariat*. The leadership of the movement was made up of demagogues and adventurers coming from all classes, while most of the fighting strength was supplied by the petty nobility and gentry who had been enrolled as officers during the 1914–18 war. The old propertied middle class followed only very slowly and reluctantly, while the new "middle class" of salaried office employees floated about in a vacuum, and eventually came down on the fascist side under the impact of mass unemployment, socialist incompetence, and the collapse of democracy. The entire phenomenon was historically unique and had no precise sequel after the 1939–45 war, which was vastly more destructive of lives and property and which completed the ruin of the old middle class and peasantry throughout wide areas of Europe. It is impossible to dissociate fascism from the nationalist movements which preceded it and which, for historical reasons, were far more virulent in Italy and Germany than in France or Britain. Causal explanations of a sociological type are too mechanical to serve as a guide. One may also suspect that they came into fashion only because Lenin was no longer there to dampen the ardor of his disciples.

The Leninist theory of imperialism proper is rather more firmly grounded. Although induced by Hobson's empirical analysis of 1902, it avoids the theoretical mistake of making capital investment abroad dependent on underconsumption at home. For Hobson, the "taproot of imperialism" was the failure of consumption to keep up with production.[18] Lack of investment opportunity at home generated a drive to extend imperial rule over dependent territories, where capital could safely and profitably be invested. Lenin rejected underconsumption as an explanation, putting in its stead Hilferding's theory of finance capital as the driving force behind expansionism and empire-building. He thus avoided the trap of having to explain why profits could be made more easily from starving peasants abroad than from relatively well-paid workers at home.[19] At the same time, however, he introduced the falling rate of profit as an explanation of the imperialist search for colonial superprofits. In point of fact, the bulk of British investment, before and after 1914, went to the developed industrial areas of Western Europe, North America, South Africa, Australia, and New Zealand, leaving the dependent tropical empire starved of investment capital. After 1945, this became the standard reproach against the historical record of British imperialism, but if one accepts it, one cannot at the same time affirm that colonial exploitation was a major source of profits for the British investor at the peak of the imperialist era. The really decisive factor in the interrelation between the metropolis and the empire was the economic development of the white-settler "dominions"—Canada, Australia, New Zealand, South Africa—through the investment of British capital. Colonial superprofits were marginal, and the annexationist drive after 1880, which led to the "scramble for Africa," is best understood as a political reaction to the threat posed by American, German, Russian, and French competition in a hypothetical future. Down to 1913, British capital still regarded the whole world as its oyster. Joseph Chamberlain's protectionist schemes were rejected precisely for this reason. As for colonial superprofits having served to corrupt the working class, British socialist historians have not been slow to point out that the years before 1914 witnessed a peak of working-class militancy.[20]

This is not to say, however, that Lenin was wrong so far as the 1920's and 1930's are concerned. His analysis stands up quite well when considered against the background of the interwar period. Paradoxically, it was less appropriate in 1916 when *Imperialism* was first drafted—for in that year the old dynastic empires of Eastern Europe were still in existence—than it was to become after 1920, when the term "empire" came to signify, above all, the British Empire and, secondly, the rival American and Japanese "co-prosperity spheres" in Latin America and East Asia respectively. If imperialism was defined to mean capital export to dependent territories plus stagnation at home, the Britain of Stanley Baldwin and Neville Chamberlain was a perfect example of the sort of thing Lenin had in mind. There was even a deliberate attempt to divert British capital investment abroad to the dependent Empire: the sort of thing Joseph Chamberlain had preached without success around 1900. In those days, the City of London and the Liberal Party proved able to defend free trade against Chamberlain's "imperialist" (that is, protectionist) assault, though he found allies among the Fabians as well as among landlords, manufacturers, and Tory die-hards. After 1918 the Liberal Party went into decline and the Conservatives became increasingly protectionist, to the point of identifying themselves quite openly with monopolist interests lying within the special protected sphere of the British Empire officially so described. This was a departure from the golden age when the entire world lay open to British manufacturers and investors. It was plainly due to increasingly stringent American, German, and Japanese competition, and to that extent it represented a defensive reaction explicable on Marxist-Leninist lines:

> British capitalism did not . . . share before 1914 the special characteristics of the German industrial structure which Lenin saw as the essence of what he called the "imperialist stage" of capitalist evolution. After 1919, however, Britain also began to exhibit more and more of these characteristics of monopoly concentration and finance-capital domination that Lenin had analyzed in Germany. Not only the growth of oligopoly, but conversion to protection from free trade and concentration on empire markets, all marked the British economy in the inter-war years. And it was increasingly in relation to the closed doors of empire trade that Germany, Italy, and Japan were challenging the "Have" powers. Britain and the other Allied powers presented a barrier to the natural development of the German economy.[21]

The "division of the world among the great international trusts" foreseen by Lenin in 1916 did in fact occur in the 1920's and 1930's. The major industries assumed a monopolistic or quasi-monopolistic structure, and the resulting giant combines entered into cartel agreements to divide the world market among them. From then on, although competition did not cease, it assumed a different form. Since the major combines normally had government support, economic and political "spheres of interest" tended to coalesce. In all these respects, the pre-1914 era could serve as a model, with the proviso that Britain had now joined by becoming a convert to protectionism. Did this result in a new form of imperialism? As we have seen, liberalism and capitalism were perfectly compatible as long as British industry dominated the world market. The partnership fell to pieces when an increasingly defensive Britain retreated behind tariff walls during the 1930's. The trouble is that no general rule can be deduced from these occurrences. Protection by its nature is of service to stagnant or declining industries, but it is also an essential element in the growth of new and highly efficient ones during their pioneering age. Bismarckian Germany in the 1880's turned protectionist not because its industries were stagnant, but because they needed a political shield behind which to prepare themselves for the coming struggle to conquer the world market. The same applies to the America of Theodore Roosevelt, whereas Franklin Roosevelt could afford to entertain his partners in 1943-45 with visions of a world thrown open to international trade on the classical liberal model. He evoked no response from Stalin, and only the most restrained enthusiasm from Winston Churchill, a former free-trader reluctantly converted to the belief that the British Empire needed tariff walls to protect itself from American competition.[22]

If protectionism can occur both at the beginning and at the close of an imperial era, the same is evidently true of militarism and navalism. Here too historical evidence discloses no correlation with either the "lowest" or the "highest" stage of economic development, but rather a random distribution of political currents making for greater or lesser aggressiveness. A good example is provided by German naval policy before 1914, which was clearly in the service of a conscious attempt to break the British stranglehold on Continental affairs. On the evidence assembled by Fritz Fischer and other historians, there is no doubt that the ruling class of Wilhelminian Germany—plus most of the liberal opposition and a substantial slice of the trade unions and the prewar Social Democrats—was fully committed to expansion overland and overseas; but the political elite was divided on the issue of challenging the British Empire. Moreover, the naval enterprise was counterproductive from the imperialist standpoint, since it brought about a coalition of Germany's enemies.[23]

Among Lenin's contemporaries, Rosa Luxemburg (1871–1919)

occupies an important place, and her *Accumulation of Capital* (1913) still holds the attention of academic economists who regard her theoretical solution of the problem as mistaken. In some respects, the book must rank as a period piece. In introducing it to a British audience in 1951, Joan Robinson at one point felt obliged to note that "On the purely analytical plane her affinity seems to be with Hobson rather than with Keynes." Considering the date, hardly a surprise. But the work has a dimension that lifts it beyond the usual range of scholastic wrangling over the reproduction schemata in the second volume of *Capital*. Rosa Luxemburg wrote about capital accumulation because she stood in need of an explanation for something that was actually going on in the Europe of her day: an arms race pointing straight to the catastrophe of 1914. In a sense she knew the answer before she had formulated her question: militarism represented an outlet for an unmanageable surplus generated in the capitalist production process. The thesis would have gained in plausibility had it been sharpened to the point of stating that, because it is wasteful and does not compete with productive forms of investment, arms expenditure creates no problems for a capitalist market economy. The issue does not emerge clearly, and a perfectly valid sociological analysis of militarism as an instrument of expansion into the preindustrial hinterland of the modern world is transformed into an unconvincing explanation of how surplus value is realized.

The true interest of the argument lies in its emphasis on capitalism's disruptive effect upon the "natural economy" of peoples not yet introduced to the blessings of a "free" market economy—its familiar "civilized" refusal to recognize the existence of human beings other than paying customers. Even if there is some extravagance in identifying "European civilization" as no more than "commodity exchange with European capital,"[24] it does no harm to be reminded that the incidental blessings of Westernization came in the wake of colonial plunder and the forcible disruption of peasant economies. From here, the road is short to a discussion of international loans and their consequences. "The imperialist phase of capitalist accumulation which implies universal competition comprises the industrialization and capitalist emancipation of the *hinterland* where capital formerly realized its surplus value. Characteristic of this phase are: lending abroad, railroad construction, revolutions, and wars."[25]

At this point Rosa Luxemburg's argument acquires a dimension lacking in the contemporary discussion of "modernization." She had grasped the point of Marx's thesis that "progress" necessarily assumes a catastrophic form: the ancient social order is violently disrupted, and capitalist industrialization unfolds in the midst of a terrifying upheaval whose meaning is concealed from the participants. The Industrial Revolution itself had been brought about by social convulsions ultimately traceable to the institution of a market economy. The latter-day global evolution of capitalism was promoted by a world-wide movement of capital from Europe to Africa and Asia. Imperialism was the process whereby the backward regions of the globe were drawn into the maelstrom that had already, in an earlier age, engulfed the ancient peasant economies of Europe. By now the transformation had come to encompass the entire globe and the resulting crises were bound up with international rivalries pointing toward an era of warfare. Her argument must be cited at some length to bring out its internal consistency, as well as its prophetic character:

> Just as the substitution of commodity economy for a natural economy, and that of capitalist production for a simple commodity production, was achieved by wars, social crises and the destruction of entire social systems, so at present the achievement of capitalist autonomy in the *hinterland* and backward colonies is attained amidst wars and revolutions. Revolution is an essential for the process of capitalist emancipation. The backward communities must shed their obsolete political organisations, relics of natural and simple commodity economy, and create a modern

state machinery adapted to the purposes of capitalist production. The revolutions in Turkey, Russia and China fall under this heading.[26]

This was written in 1912, when the only revolutions in Turkey, Russia, and China were still safely bourgeois. Rosa Luxemburg had before her eyes the fumbling Young Turk regime from which in due course the Kemalist dictatorship was to emerge in the 1920's; the Russian upheaval of 1905–7, which had instituted a semblance of parliamentary government, complete with political parties and an uncensored press; and the fall of the Manchu dynasty in China. All three came under the heading of what would nowadays be hailed by liberals as "modernization." To Luxemburg, trained as a Marxist to see the catastrophic side of the process, these events heralded a series of further upheavals, for the newly emerging capitalist economies in the formerly backward countries could function only under the shield of a "modern state machinery." That the state was primarily a war machine was something she did not have to be told by Clausewitz's successors who, in 1912, were busy preparing Germany for the great contest. Marx and Engels had entertained no doubts on the subject. Hence, the "imperialist phase of capitalist accumulation"—precisely because it had become global—was bound to promote imperialist wars.

Hobson and Hilferding, in their different ways, had anticipated this line of reasoning, but Luxemburg synthesized Hobson's empirical description with Hilferding's theoretical analysis. At times, the result sounds startlingly "modern": "Imperialism is the political expression of the accumulation of capital in its competitive struggle for what remains still open of the noncapitalist environment."[27] This may stand as an example of the manner in which a theorist intuitively hits upon an important discovery by way of unsound premises and faulty reasoning. The passage concludes with a piece of apocalyptic rhetoric: "Though imperialism is the historical method for prolonging the career of capitalism, it is also a sure means of bringing it to a swift conclusion . . . the mere tendency towards imperialism of itself takes forms which make the final phase of capitalism a period of catastrophe." Why only the final phase? And where is the evidence that the imperialist phase represents finality?

Imperial Germany before 1914 was a country where the drive toward the creation of an economically self-sufficient *Mitteleuropa* could not be overlooked, and Luxemburg duly pounced on its leading theorists. Those Bismarckian conservatives who styled themselves, or were styled by others, *Kathedersozialisten* (socialists of the chair—meaning the academic chair) had by 1900 become not only protectionists but economic autarchists. In other words, they were on the road to empire in the modern bourgeois sense of the term, complete with "geopolitics" and resentful sideglances at the "three Empires" (Great Britain, Russia, and the United States) already in existence. From there it was only a short step to the demand that Germany acquire a navy strong enough to break the British stranglehold, and thus become, if not a world power, at least a desirable ally of the Big Three. Schmoller led the chorus, while insisting that it was Germany's high task to see to it that, in the twentieth century, the "Three Empires" should not subject the remainder of the world to "a brutal neo-mercantilism." Rosa Luxemburg noted all this and was properly sarcastic about it. At the same time, she virtually adopted the classical liberal argument that capitalism was a world system, hence not subject to "the bookish decrees issued by German scholars" enamored of national autarchy. On the same grounds, she dismissed out of hand Struve's suggestion that a country possessing a sufficiently large territory and population could turn itself into a self-contained whole. Struve, who had once been a Marxist, was clearly thinking of his native Russia. To Luxemburg, writing in 1912, he was a latter-day *Narodnik* who did not understand the operation of capitalism as a global system that automatically subordinated all national units to its infernal logic. There is some reason to believe that Trotsky, who possessed no grasp of economics, derived from Luxemburg his obstinate conviction that "socialism in one country" was not merely reactionary but unworkable for economic reasons alone. If so, Luxemburg may have been responsible for equipping the Trotskyist movement with a universalist perspective which made better sense in the liberal age than in the political reality of a neomercantilist era.

Before turning to Schumpeter's alternative explanation of imperialism, which was couched in the form of a running commentary on the Austro-Marxist doctrine produced by Otto Bauer and Rudolf Hilferding, one further side excursion—this time into Keynes's work—is necessary. As Keynes's disquisitions on the topic are, in the main, confined to his rather circumspect praise of the mercantilists—already noted in an earlier chapter—this excursion will be brief. Being a critic of Alfred Marshall and his pupils, Keynes did not believe the market economy could stay in equilibrium without state intervention. It was this departure from orthodoxy that led him to re-evaluate the mercantilists and it is this alone in his work which has any bearing on the question of imperialism. For the rest, his *General Theory* does not touch on our subject or on the wider issues of technological change and industrialization. This leads to a more general observation, which is likely to give offense in Anglo-American academic quarters: Continental Europeans (professional economists included) have some trouble with the notion that in the 1930's there occurred a cataclysmic event known as the "Keynesian revolution." No such volcanic disturbance ever came to their attention, either before or after 1945. What they noted was that, if the 1939–45 war instituted full employment in the West, rearmament had already done as much for Germany between 1933 and 1939. Thereafter, all Western governments, for political reasons, were clearly unwilling to let unemployment mount to crisis proportions. In Eastern Europe no such problem arose since industrialization under conditions of total state ownership left no room for the uncontrolled play of market forces. But

these forces were in any case never allowed to work themselves
out "freely" in the West either—not even in West Germany or
Japan, where the economy was anyhow kept going by a colossal
export boom. For some reason, no one in authority in these
countries ever found it necessary to invoke Keynes in support of
full-employment policies, which were quite simply accepted as
a political necessity. What the Europeans did notice was that
the country where Keynes enjoyed the highest reputation—
Britain—also had the worst economic record.[28]

If Keynes had by 1935 come to equivocate on the topic of
mercantilism—and by implication on that of economic nationalism and state intervention to insure adequate capital investment
at home—Schumpeter, writing in 1919 under the impact of the
Anglo-German conflict that had culminated in the war of 1914–
18, plainly intended *Imperialism and Social Classes*[29] (which
had been drafted during the war years) to serve as a tract for the
times: specifically as a warning to the Germans not to relapse
into the political follies which had laid them low. But the essay
also had a theoretical content, impartially aimed at protectionist
conservatives on the Right and the Bauer-Hilferding school of
Marxism on the Left. It does not deal with Lenin, whose
pamphlet on imperialism became available in German only in
1920. Schumpeter in 1919 was still carrying on the prewar debate.
It was of the essence of his position that capitalism could get on
very well without imperialism. This of course was the traditional
liberal faith, but Schumpeter added something new and original
—an analysis of imperialism as the outgrowth of prebourgeois
forms of social life. Imperialism was not merely retrogressive
from a laissez faire standpoint: it was quite specifically linked
with the survival of ancient and outdated modes of thought
anchored in the existence of social strata whose political hegemony had shaped the world of the emerging *bourgeoisie*.

> Whoever seeks to understand Europe must not overlook that
> even today its life, its ideology, its politics are greatly under the
> influence of the feudal "substance," that while the *bourgeoisie*

can assert its interests everywhere, it "rules" only in exceptional circumstances, and then only briefly. The bourgeois outside his office and the professional man of capitalism outside his profession cut a very sorry figure. Their spiritual leader is the rootless "intellectual," a slender reed open to every impulse and a prey to unrestrained emotionalism. The "feudal" elements, on the other hand, have both feet on the ground, even psychologically speaking. Their ideology is as stable as their mode of life. . . . This quality of possessing a definite character and cast of mind as a class . . . extends their power far beyond their actual bases. . . .

Imperialist absolutism has patterned not only the economy of the *bourgeoisie* but also its mind—in the interests of autocracy and against those of the *bourgeoisie* itself. This significant dichotomy in the bourgeois mind—which in part explains its wretched weakness in politics, culture, and life generally, earns it the understandable contempt of the Left and the Right, and proves the accuracy of our diagnosis—is best exemplified by two phenomena that are very close to our subject: present-day nationalism and militarism. . . .

Nationalism and militarism, while not creatures of capitalism, become "capitalized" and in the end draw their best energies from capitalism. Capitalism involves them in its workings and thereby keeps them alive, politically as well as economically. And they, in turn, affect capitalism, cause it to deviate from the course it might have followed alone, support many of its interests.[30]

If only the European *bourgeoisie* had known its own interests, it would have avoided the imperialist madness leading to 1914–18! This was virtually what Kautsky had suggested in 1914–15 and what had made Lenin so angry. It is difficult not to feel that Schumpeter juggles with the term "imperialism." True, the European middle class had grown up within an absolutist framework, allowed the landed nobility to run the government for it, and even propped up the dynastic empires of the Hohenzollerns, Habsburgs, and Romanovs. But that same middle class had by 1914 spawned a plutocratic upper stratum which coalesced with the ruling elites of the ancient monarchies and rendered them more, rather than less, aggressive and expansionist. Schumpeter's ingenious apology made good sense for his native Austria-Hungary, but then the Habsburg monarchy was a political anachronism. There was nothing weak or contemptible about great German industrialists like Walter Rathenau, or for that matter great scholars like Max Weber—an archexponent of nationalism and imperialism both before and after 1918.

Moreover, Schumpeter undercut his own position by taking over the laissez faire argument and then reluctantly conceding the validity of the Marxist thesis concerning the link between protectionism, monopoly capitalism, and external aggression. First, the restatement of classical liberal orthodoxy: "It may be stated as being beyond controversy that where free trade prevails, *no* class has an interest in forcible expansion as such."[31] And, "since protectionism is not an essential characteristic of the capitalist economy—otherwise the English national economy would scarcely be capitalist—it is apparent that any economic interest in forcible expansion on the part of a people or a class is not necessarily a product of capitalism."[32] Unfortunately, protectionism does exist and has nefarious consequences, especially when combined with the drive toward monopoly: "under free trade only *international* cartels would be possible," and Schumpeter regards them as harmless, since under such conditions "there would be conflicts in economic interests neither among different nations nor among the corresponding classes of different nations."[33] "A protectionist policy, however, does facilitate the formation of cartels and trusts. And it is true that this circumstance thoroughly alters the alignment of interests. It was neo-Marxist doctrine that first tellingly described this causal connection (Bauer) and fully recognized the significance of the 'functional change in protectionism' (Hilferding)."[34] The change comes about because trusts and cartelized industries protected by tariff walls establish monopoly prices at home, while dumping their surplus output abroad, in some cases below cost; the consequence is "a conflict of interests between nations that becomes so sharp that it cannot be overcome by the existing basic community of interests."[35]

This conclusion does not seem very far removed from the Marxist position, at least in its Austrian version; and yet Schumpeter insists that "Imperialism . . . is atavistic in character. It falls into that large group of surviving features from earlier ages that play such an important part in every concrete social situation."[36] For the same reason he is convinced that imperialism cannot win a substantial working-class following: "Social imperialism in the sense of imperialist interests on the part of the workers, interests to which an imperialist attitude ought to correspond, if the workers only understood it correctly—such an imperialist policy oriented toward working-class interests is nonsensical. *A people's imperialism is today an impossibility*."[37] On Schumpeter's assumptions, as stated in 1919, Italian and German fascism are inexplicable. His pupils might argue that both terminated in disaster. But this does not alter the fact that a "people's imperialism" was just what the Italian and German working classes—or anyway the bulk of them—came to believe in for a time. European politics in the 1920's and 1930's are not analyzable in terms of prebourgeois survivals, although these "residues" played a part in determining the tolerance with which the ancient nobility and gentry viewed plebeian demagogues playing at Caesarism. Certainly these declining classes threw their weight behind fascism, but when all is said and done the historian has to register the uncomfortable fact that no class proved immune to the infection. The matter can be stated in fairly simple terms: as long as the European *bourgeoisie* retained its faith in liberal democracy, the working class did the same (albeit in the shape of social-democratic reformism); when the middle class turned fascist, the working class followed suit. Had it been otherwise, the Third Reich could never have waged war as it did.[38]

Notes

1. For the theoretical background of such utterances, see Paul A. Baran, *The Political Economy of Growth* (New York: Monthly Review Press, 1957), *passim;* Paul A. Baran and Paul M. Sweezy, *Monopoly Capital* (New York: Monthly Review Press, 1966; London: Penguin Books, 1968), *passim.*

2. For a new edition, see V. I. Lenin, *Selected Works,* vol. 1 (Moscow: Progress Publishers, 1967), pp. 675 ff. The pamphlet was passed by the Czarist censor in 1916 and appeared legally before the February Revolution of 1917. The new preface, dated "Petrograd, April 26, 1917," draws attention to this fact, and also asks the reader to "substitute Russia for Japan, and Finland, Poland, Courland, the Ukraine, Khiva, Bokhara, Estonia, or other regions peopled by non-Great Russians, for Korea"—Japan's annexation of Korea having been mentioned in the text as an example of imperialist annexation, so as not to alarm the censor. Mention of the Ukraine must have set some readers wondering about the relevance of Lenin's analysis of modern monopoly capitalism to more primitive forms of territorial annexation. For Rosa Luxemburg's theory of imperialism, see *The Accumulation of Capital* (London: Routledge, 1951; New York: St. Martin, 2d ed., 1965), with an Introduction by Joan Robinson. For the general theme, see (among others) Paul M. Sweezy, *The Theory of Capitalist Development* (New York: Oxford University Press, 1942; London: Dennis Dobson, 1946), pp. 190 ff., 202 ff., 254 ff. It may be noteworthy that Lenin paid no attention to Rosa Luxemburg, basing himself instead on J. A. Hobson and on Rudolf Hilferding's great work *Das Finanzkapital* (Vienna, 1910; Moscow, 1912). See also N. Bukharin, *Der Imperialismus und die Akkumulation des Kapitals* (Vienna and Berlin: Verlag für Literatur und Politik, 1926).

3. J. A. Hobson, *Imperialism: A Study* (1902; rev. ed., London: Allen & Unwin, 1948; Ann Arbor: University of Michigan Press, 1965), p. 106.

4. Lenin, *Selected Works,* vol. 1, p. 742.

5. *Ibid.,* pp. 768 ff.

6. *Ibid.,* p. 770.

7. *Ibid.,* p. 740.

8. V. I. Lenin, "The War and Russian Social-Democracy," written in September–October, 1914 and first published in *Sotsial-Democrat,* no. 33 (November 1, 1914); reprinted in Lenin, *Selected Works,* vol. 1, pp. 657 ff.; see also *Collected Works,* vol. 21. The article concludes with the words: "Long live the international fraternity of the workers against the chauvinism and patriotism of the *bourgeoisie* of all countries! Long live a proletarian International, freed from opportunism!" No mention of the peasantry, then as ever the principal reservoir of "bourgeois" patriotism.

9. Lenin, *Selected Works*, vol. 1, p. 679.

10. *Ibid.*, p. 680.

11. Karl Marx and Friedrich Engels, *Werke*, vol. 17 (East Berlin, 1962), pp. 271 ff.; vol. 22 (East Berlin, 1963), pp. 30 ff. See in particular Engels's detailed forecast in the article he published in Kautsky's *Neue Zeit* of May, 1890 where among other things he wrote: "The German annexation turns France into Russia's ally against Germany, the Tsarist threat to Constantinople turns Austria, even Italy, into allies of Germany. Both sides prepare themselves for a decisive struggle, a war such as the world has never seen, in which ten or fifteen million combatants will .oppose each other in arms. Only two factors have until now prevented the outbreak of this terrible conflict: the unprecedented progress in arms technology, which supersedes every new rifle model by new inventions before even one army can introduce it; and secondly, the absolute incalculability of the chances, the total uncertainty as to who will finally emerge victorious from this gigantic struggle. This whole danger of world war will disappear on the day when a change of affairs in Russia enables the Russian people to terminate the traditional annexationist policy of its Tsars, and to concern itself with its own highly endangered vital interests, instead of pursuing fantasies of world domination."

12. Lenin, *Selected Works*, vol. 1, pp. 680–81.

13. *Ibid.*, p. 683.

14. Lenin, "Better fewer, but better," in *Selected Works*, vol. 3 (Moscow: Progress Publishers, 1967), p. 785. See also *Collected Works*, vol. 33.

15. For documentation on the later and more dramatic phase of the Sino–Soviet dispute, see the special issue of *Studies in Comparative Communism* (Los Angeles: University of Southern California, July–October, 1969); for the historical and theoretical background see Hélène Carrère d'Encausse and Stuart R. Schram, *Marxism and Asia* (London: Allen Lane The Penguin Press, 1969), esp. pp. 317 ff. Also Stuart R. Schram, *The Political Thought of Mao Tse-tung* (1963; rev. ed., London: Penguin Books; New York: Praeger, 1969). The dichotomy socialism-imperialism, with the Soviet Union and the Communist movement representing the former, is particularly marked in such utterances as Mao's congratulatory oration "Stalin is our commander," originally a birthday tribute in December, 1939, but still published a decade later after the Chinese revolution had carried the Communist party to power. See Schram, *The Political Thought of Mao Tse-tung*, pp. 426–27: "On the one side is imperialism which represents the front of the oppressors. On the other side is socialism, which represents the front of resistance to oppression." For all its naivety, this formulation was still rooted in that aspect of the Leninist inheritance which enabled Mao to identify nationalism with anti-imperialism, and both with socialism. In 1939 Stalin was hailed as "the savior of all the oppressed." Three decades later his heirs in the Kremlin had come to rank as imperialists and allies of the United States.

16. Sweezy, *The Theory of Capitalist Development*, p. 329.

17. *Ibid.*, p. 333.

18. Hobson, *Imperialism*, pp. 81–83.

19. Michael Barratt Brown, *After Imperialism* (London: Heinemann; New York: Hillary House, 1963), p. 96. This argument cannot be countered by dwelling on the superprofits of oil monopolies and capitalist investments in mines or plantations. Hobson had quite specifically asserted that the economic drive behind imperialism was the shrinkage of domestic markets for consumer goods. The implication was that such markets could be built up in the dependent tropical empire, whereas in fact they existed and expanded in the white-settler "dominions" which also became a major outlet for British capital investment.

20. *Ibid.*, p. 101. See also p. 99: "It is true that by 1913 nearly a tenth of the national income was accounted for by payments received from overseas investments . . . and this formed perhaps a quarter of all property incomes. Only about a sixth of this could, however, be said to come from India and the other dependent colonies; the very much greater part came . . . from the other developing industrial lands, the United States, European countries, and the independent British dominions."

21. *Ibid.*, p. 121.

22. Gabriel Kolko, *The Politics of War: Allied Diplomacy and the World Crisis of 1943–1945* (London: Weidenfeld & Nicolson; New York: Random House, 1969), pp. 242 ff., 280 ff. This learned work is more useful for its assessment of U.S. economic policy than for its rather uncertain treatment of European affairs, a topic that demands a different approach. Where Kolko scores is in analyzing the Anglo–American relationship, which was one of fundamental rivalry overlaid by the necessities of wartime cooperation: in this respect resembling the Anglo–Dutch alliance of an earlier era, with the weaker partner inevitably winding up in the role of satellite.

23. See Jonathan Steinberg, "The Kaiser's Navy and German Society," *Past & Present*, no. 28 (July, 1964): 103: "The first, and most disagreeable, of these insights for German historians must be that the Imperial German Navy failed to accomplish its objectives in war; the second that it contributed more than any other German organization to the disruption of the peace before 1914; the third that both its failures in war and its behavior in peace reflected the values, attitudes, and ideas of the German middle class, the class to which the great majority of historians belonged." The enterprise was largely irrational and promoted by Pan-German fantasies which had seized hold of the German middle class in the Bismarck era, and were then taken up and promoted by William II and his advisers as a means of providing the Monarchy with a popular following. See Hartmut Pogge von Strandmann, "Domestic Origins of Germany's Colonial Expansion under Bismarck," *Past & Present*, no. 42 (February, 1969): 140 ff. Similar considerations apply to the frequently irrational, not to say lunatic, behavior of the Japanese military and naval leaders between 1931 and 1941.

24. Luxemburg, *The Accumulation of Capital*, p. 387.

25. *Ibid.*, p. 419.

26. *Idem.*

27. *Ibid.*, p. 446; see also the note on Schmoller on pp. 295–96 of the work.

28. See J. A. Schumpeter, "John Maynard Keynes," in *Ten Great Economists: From Marx to Keynes* (London: Allen & Unwin, 1952; New York: Oxford University Press, 1951). For the standard liberal treatment of the topic see Robert Lekachman, *The Age of Keynes* (London: Allen Lane The Penguin Press, 1967; New York: Random House, 1966). The author does not fail to note that the age of Keynes was also the age of Lytton Strachey, but it is possible to feel that he gives insufficient weight to the fact. See also Robert Lekachman, ed., *Keynes and the Classics* (Boston: D. C. Heath, 1964); Michael Stewart, *Keynes and After* (London: Penguin Books, 1967; Baltimore: Penguin Books, 1968).

29. First published under the title "Zur Soziologie der Imperialismen" in the *Archiv für Sozialwissenschaft und Sozial politik,* vol. 46 (1919), issued in book form the same year and now available in an English translation in Paul M. Sweezy, ed., *Imperialism and Social Classes* (Oxford: Basil Blackwell, 1951), together with a later essay on social classes, likewise published in the *Archiv,* vol. 57 (1927), of which Schumpeter had by then become an editor. The theme of the second essay had been outlined by Schumpeter as early as 1910–11, and was later presented by him at Columbia University in lecture form in 1913–14. Both essays can be regarded as contributions to a discussion which, in Austria anyway, had been initiated by the Marxist school; in Britain, it dated back to the Boer War of 1899–1902, Chamberlain's protectionist campaign, and Hobson's restatement of classical liberalism.

30. "Imperialism and Capitalism," in Sweezy, *Imperialism and Social Classes,* pp. 122–28.

31. *Ibid.*, p. 99.

32. *Ibid.*, p. 101.

33. *Ibid.*, p. 100.

34. *Ibid.*, p. 104.

35. *Ibid.*, p. 105.

36. *Ibid.*, p. 84.

37. *Ibid.*, p. 115.

38. F. L. Carsten, *The Rise of Fascism* (London: Batsford; Berkeley, Calif.: University of California Press, 1967), *passim.*

CHAPTER 8

From Marx to Mao

AMONG NEW RECRUITS ADHERING TO THE RADICAL LEFT, the term "imperialism" is currently employed interchangeably to designate four quite different kinds of relationships which Lenin had been careful to distinguish: (1) national oppression of the sort practiced in the old dynastic East European empires before 1914–18; (2) colonialism of the Anglo-Indian type during and after the mercantilist era; (3) "liberal imperialism," classically represented by the British and subsequently the American drive to throw foreign markets open to Western capital; (4) the transfer of surplus value from the poor countries to the rich through trade relationships which in practice discriminate against undeveloped economies. By running these different meanings together one can achieve startling rhetorical effects without coming any closer to a genuine theory of imperialism. Types (1) and (2) are historically outmoded, which is not to say that national oppression of minorities has vanished; on the contrary, it is widespread, notably in African and Asian countries recently emancipated from the European yoke. Types (3) and (4) are currently the target of widespread denunciation, both in Anglo-American literature and among radical nationalists in the Third World.[1]

134

In the great age of Marxist economic writing, between 1910 and 1930, theories of capitalist imperialism were worked out by Hilferding, Luxemburg, Lenin, Bukharin, and others, with the intention of differentiating the topic from the more general subject of dynastic expansion and national oppression: the former being rooted in the feudal age, the latter too familiar to lend itself to theoretical treatment and anyhow not a suitable theme for economic analysis. Of the remaining types, emphasis has in recent years increasingly shifted from (3) to (4), with liberals and socialists putting forward rival explanations of what has caused uneven development within a world economy dominated by the industrial-capitalist nexus. In its latest transmogrification the debate has been further enriched by the Maoist thesis that there exists a form of socialist imperialism represented by the Soviet Union, though oddly enough this phenomenon is supposed to have made its appearance only since the demise of Stalin in 1953. Much of this literature, while scholarly in appearance, is in fact propagandist, and the same applies to the productions of the liberal-imperialist school.[2]

If confusion is to be avoided, it seems desirable to eliminate types (1) and (2) from the agenda, with the obvious proviso that even revolutionary nationalism may become the breeding ground of expansionism. Whether one chooses to describe this familiar phenomenon as imperialism is strictly a semantic matter. If, in the ancient democratic tradition which Marx and Engels inherited from their predecessors, one identifies imperialism with national oppression, then the present-day Soviet Union does not differ greatly in some respects from the Empire of the Romanovs. This would certainly be the opinion of the citizens of Czechoslovakia, and probably of most East Europeans, including not a few Communists. Support for this unflattering conclusion can be found in Lenin's writings, which is why their interpretation has become a very awkward matter for the present rulers of what is officially styled the Soviet Union. But we do not advance the discussion of Marxist theory by making the obvious point that

Lenin and others recognized a distinction between traditional and specifically modern types of imperialism. At most this procedure makes it easier to account for the existence of (a) capitalism without empire and (b) empire without capitalism. The former has become typical of contemporary Western Europe; the latter appears to be a fairly accurate description of the Soviet Union plus its East European client states. Since imperialism is older than capitalism, there seems to be no particular reason why, for theoretical purposes, the two should not be dissociated, to the point perhaps of laying the groundwork of an as yet nonexistent theory of post-capitalist imperialism. Such a theory, if and when it comes into being, will have to take the Stalinist era for its starting point. What it will look like remains to be seen, but it seems improbable that the analysis of market relations will figure prominently within it.

A Marxist theory of capitalist imperialism must in any case take for its starting point Marx's well-known dictum "The real barrier of capitalist production is capital itself." Marx goes on to say:

> It is that capital and its self-expansion appear as the starting and the closing point, the motive and the purpose of production; that production is only production for *capital* and not vice versa, the means of production are not mere means for a constant expansion of the living process of the *society* of producers. . . . The means—unconditional development of the productive forces of society—comes continually into conflict with the limited purpose, the self-expansion of the existing capital. The capitalist mode of production is for this reason a historical means of developing the material forces of production and creating an appropriate world market, and is at the same time a continual conflict between this its historical task and its own corresponding relations of social production.[3]

Viewed from some such perspective, the phenomenon of imperialism loses its seeming irrationality, although this does not exclude specific irrationalities which in retrospect appear as gigantic political follies or miscalculations. Thus, as we have seen, it is arguable that on any rational calculation of chances the behavior of the German and Japanese ruling groups in the first half of this century was self-defeating. Circumstances of this kind certainly demand an explanation, but the latter falls into the province of the historian. On an over-all view, imperialism makes sense, at any rate for the hegemonial power in control of the system during a given epoch. At the same time, imperialism acts as a brake upon the economic development of regions controlled—directly or indirectly—by the metropolis, and to that extent it constitutes a barrier to capitalist expansion, inasmuch as it interferes with the growth of precisely those external markets which investors and exporters are in search of.

The contradiction was apparent to Marx, although in his major work he gave no systematic attention to it. His occasional comments on British imperialism in India anticipate some aspects of later controversies among British and other socialists; for example, "England has to fulfill a double mission in India: one destructive, the other regenerating—the annihilation of [the] old Asiatic society, and the laying of the material foundations of Western society in Asia."[4] This is followed by the observation that the British cannot plunder India without at the same time helping to industrialize it. "They intend now drawing a net of railroads over India. And they will do it. The results must be inappreciable." "I know that the English millocracy intend to endow India with railways with the exclusive view of extracting at diminished expenses the cotton and other raw materials for their manufactures. But when you have once introduced machinery into the locomotion of a country which possesses iron and coal, you are unable to withhold it from its fabrication. You cannot maintain a net of railways over an immense country without introducing all those industrial processes necessary to meet the immediate and current wants of railway locomotion, and out of which there must grow the application of machinery to those branches of industry not immediately connected with railways.

The railway system will therefore become, in India, truly the forerunner of modern industry. . . . Modern industry, resulting from the railway system, will dissolve the hereditary divisions of labor upon which rest the Indian castes, those decisive impediments to Indian progress and Indian power. . . . At all events, we may safely expect to see, at a more or less remote period, the regeneration of that great and interesting country."[5]

Modern economic historians have noted that Marx expected too much from Indian railroad construction, which in the event opened up a market for British rather than for Indian manufacturers. This does not invalidate the general point he wished to make about the impact of industrial capitalism on backward and dependent countries: "The bourgeois period of history has to create the material basis of the new world—on the one hand the universal intercourse founded upon the mutual dependency of mankind, and the means of that intercourse; on the other hand the development of the productive powers of man and the transformation of material production into a scientific domination of natural agencies."[6] The argument is in tune with a line of reasoning developed five years earlier in the *Communist Manifesto* concerning the revolutionary role of the *bourgeoisie* in pioneering a new mode of production. One may say that Marx regarded laissez faire rather than protection as the "classical" form of capitalist trade relations, and liberal imperialism—the imperialism of free trade—as its political counterpart. The protectionist movement in Britain after 1900—a movement which obtained support from prominent Fabians as well as from the "geopoliticians" of the political Right—would have struck him as an aberration or alternatively as a symptom of decline. On this issue, since there was no Marxist literature worth mentioning in Britain before the 1930's, the cosmopolitan tradition—and the concurrent critique of protectionist imperialism as parasitic and retrograde—was left to radical liberals such as Hobson. Social-imperialist propaganda for the most part appealed to conservative sentiment in a milieu where it merged with Social

Darwinism. Its socialist, or pseudosocialist, fellow-travelers in some cases blossomed out as precursors of fascism.[7]

Because the political battle lines were drawn in this manner, it is easy to overlook the fact that the system the Liberal Party, and subsequently the Labour Party, defended down to 1932 —when free trade was abandoned—guaranteed Britain's preeminent world position as an exporter of both capital and commodities. "The advantage of the strategic lines of the empire was the preservation of a world of free trade."[8] The muddle into which writers like Hobson got themselves on this issue was due to their tendency to identify imperialism with colonialism. Their American contemporaries and successors did the same, with the result that public attention was focused upon U.S. control of the Philippines, or of some minor Latin American republic, while the far more important issue of North America's increasingly central position within the global division of labor was ignored. In retrospect, it is clear that the era of British predominance was governed by a set of relationships which, from the 1930's onward and more particularly after 1945, became a model for the U.S. policy-makers, especially those among them who quite sincerely saw themselves serving the cause of universal free trade, as against the benighted protectionism of the British—not to mention the Axis powers who had gone to war for the stated purpose of carving out exclusive "spheres of influence" for themselves at the expense of everyone else:

> Free trade was the instrument of Britain's industrial supremacy holding back development elsewhere; this condition would, in the end, have checked British growth too, as foreign markets were impoverished. But British capital investment in Europe and North America, and in other lands of European settlement, created the necessary expanding markets for manufactured exports. In the not so long run, it created also new competitors for British industry.[9]

If the dissolution of the "visible" British Empire after 1945 did not have the disastrous consequences often predicted by Con-

servative politicians, at least one important explanation has to
do with the fact that capital and labor had in the past pre-
dominantly moved to lands of European settlement. Elsewhere,
power was normally transferred to governments which, by and
large, did not expropriate Western capital assets. This was partly
a consequence of the Soviet-American rivalry which, from 1945
onward, established new political alignments cutting across the
simple antagonism of colonizers and colonized. But it also represented an option on the part of nationalist elites intent on
industrializing their respective countries with the aid of European, American, and Soviet investments alike. The cold war was,
from the standpoint of these elites, a means of extracting aid
from the industrial powers, whether capitalist or nominally
socialist. This applies to the greatest of the newly emancipated
countries, India, as much as it does to the small states formerly
belonging to the French colonial empire in Africa.

American policy was predictably modeled on the British
example. Free trade having become the official ideology of the
United States after 1945, it was only natural that a treaty em-
bodying laissez faire principles should have been negotiated by
Washington with the Kuomintang Government in November,
1946.[10] Hence in part the traumatic shock induced three years
later by the so-called loss of China. Hence also the quixotic
determination to keep the Chiang Kai-shek regime going, at least
on Formosa. What one needs to guard against is the notion that
it made economic sense after 1949 for the U.S. Government to
boycott mainland China instead of entering into trade relations
with it. People who adopt this line of reasoning have transformed Marxism into economic determinism of the crudest kind.
Specifically, they fail to see that, in relation to China, both
American and Russian policies were and are inevitably governed
by balance-of-power considerations. The Chinese revolution was
perceived as a menace to America's world position and opposed
on those grounds, as a matter of principle and not because the
Chinese market was of overwhelming importance to U.S. ex-

porters. When the aggravation of the Sino-Soviet conflict—itself inexplicable on Leninist grounds—diminished the prevailing fear of a monolithic Communist bloc, Washington showed itself ready to improve relations with mainland China. It is perfectly true that, from the official U.S. standpoint, the Maoist regime represented a barrier to that unrestricted flow of trade and capital investment which the liberal ideology postulates as the optimal condition to be sought by policy-makers. But in an imperfect world even a state-controlled economy can become a trading partner for the United States, and Maoist determination to industrialize without foreign aid at least relieves Washington of one standing source of embarrassment: the need to subsidize another country's modernization. As for the West European countries, it should not be necessary to emphasize that an embargo on trade with China could never be anything but a nuisance to them.[11]

A tendency to identify imperialism with colonialism is marked at both ends of the political spectrum in the United States: among liberals who reproduce Hobson's mistaken emphasis upon protectionist control of tropical markets and raw materials, and among adherents of the New Left who see corporate power lurking behind every bush, thus causing the U.S. Government to intervene in Asian and Latin American countries so as to forestall or suppress national revolutions menacing the sources of corporate profit. If these military incursions were to become marginal to the "invisible" hegemony of the United States within the global division of labor, the adherents of both schools would be deprived of a precious argument: the liberals would no longer be able to celebrate the beneficial effects of capital investment in backward areas, and the New Left would be hard put to explain how the corporations keep going, even though they have to compromise with nationalist regimes abroad. The kind of relationship currently subsisting between France and the North African countries could easily reproduce itself in areas formally independent of the United States and already sufficiently autonomous to expropriate U.S. capital assets—with or without compensation. If this were to occur on a substantial scale, with the tacit connivance of U.S. policy-makers no longer hypnotized by fear of "world Communism," it would not alter the hegemonial position of the United States within the North Atlantic region, which is anyhow the principal field of U.S. capital investment. In short, it would leave the "imperialism of free trade" intact and in perfect economic health.

There is evidently a distinction to be drawn between U.S. capital investment in Canada or Western Europe, and the flow of such investment to undeveloped regions for the purpose of stimulating the production of oil and other raw materials required by the North American economy. In the former case, U.S. capital flows into mature industrial economies which also happen to be quite efficient competitors in third markets, and even in the U.S. domestic market. In the case of the undeveloped country, the chief beneficiaries are extractive industries which may or may not provide the economy with a surplus for industrialization. If industrialization is artificially held back, the relationship is of the semicolonial type and in due course is likely to generate nationalist resentments sufficient to unseat the local oligarchy. If this does not occur, and if a state of dependency upon the imperial metropolis is perpetuated by political or other means, then the country in question cannot become an important market for U.S. industries producing exportable goods. This pattern may perpetuate itself in marginal cases, but it can hardly become the rule without undercutting the rationale of the whole process. Fully developed industrial countries cannot be controlled by outsiders and they provide the principal markets for U.S. exports and capital alike. Undeveloped regions either remain in that state, in which case their significance must shrink, or else sufficient revenue is generated by foreign and local investment to stimulate more rapid all-round development. In that case, the relationship, while still unequal, loses its colonial character. Nor does it follow that development does not occur because more wealth is siphoned out in profits than is put in by the investors. Between 1870 and 1914, Britain clearly profited from capital exports—or else they would not have been undertaken. Income received in various forms from foreign investments was substantially larger than the net export of British capital: some £4,000 million against £2,400 million. The same is true, on an even larger scale, of U.S. investments since 1945. But some development nonetheless takes place, even though it does so merely as a by-product of capitalist profit-making.

Given the dominant position of the United States within the world market in general and the North Atlantic area in particular, it is perhaps not surprising that the current controversy over the problems and prospects of the American Empire should revive some aspects of the earlier British debate. In addition to the conservative-liberal quarrel over protectionism versus free trade, there is the quasi-Marxist interpretation of American imperialism in terms derived from Lenin's analysis of European monopoly capitalism fifty years ago. Until about 1930 that analysis was more relevant to Germany than to Britain; since 1960, it has once more ceased to fit the facts, for British capitalism has survived the loss of its colonial empire without major trouble. Conversely, West German and Japanese capitalism are thoroughly monopolistic, so that once more the equation "monopoly capitalism = colonial imperialism" has ceased to fit. On the other hand, it seems to fit the United States, provided one accepts the view that Latin America is *de facto* controlled by U.S. capital, and that its nominally independent governments stand in a semicolonial relationship to the imperial metropolis. How far this argument can be pushed, in view of Cuba's successful defiance of the North American colossus, and the growth of nationalist tendencies elsewhere in the hemisphere, is a question of some relevance to Maoists, though not to Marxists who are unable to accept Lenin's drastically simplified exposition of Hilferding's argument.

What happens, for example, if industrialization gets under

way in parts of Latin America with substantial U.S. assistance—
public and private—in the interest of creating mass consumer
markets for U.S. exports? On theoretical grounds, such a development cannot be excluded. If it is blocked by political short-
sightedness or corporate stupidity, then the resulting tensions
can in principle be resolved without altering the basic nature of
the nexus linking North and South America (omitting Cuba, which
is kept afloat by Soviet aid for political reasons). If it be said that
U.S. corporate investment will siphon out more than is put in,
the answer is that nothing but purely political considerations
forbids nationalist regimes in Latin America from stopping this
reverse flow, or even from seizing major U.S. assets, as in some
cases they have already done with complete impunity. Alternatively, if it is maintained that the countries in question will be
prevented from embarking upon all-round development, then
it follows that they cannot become important markets for U.S.
mass-production industries; in which case the issue becomes a
domestic one for U.S. interests—including the unions, as well as
the exporters—to argue out among themselves, and we are back
once more·with the familiar quarrel between conservatives and
liberals, with organized labor for the most part enlisted on the
liberal side. What, if anything, this has to do with the Leninist
equation, it is difficult to understand.

The analysis of modern capitalism in such works as Baran's
Political Economy of Growth (1957) or Baran's and Sweezy's
Monopoly Capital (1966), continues a line of reasoning pioneered by Lenin half a century ago. This may be the reason why
these authors and their followers tend to fasten on the growth
of corporate power, or on safe topics such as Japan's successful
industrialization rather than India's miserable record.[12] When
all that can be said on these themes has been exhausted, we are
no nearer an understanding of the mechanism that keeps the
system going, both in the presence and in the absense of colonial
or semicolonial patterns of dependence. If the possession of
colonies makes no difference to a flourishing capitalism, then

what is the relevance of imperialism to an up-to-date theory of how capitalist profit is realized under monopolistic conditions? A plausible answer might be that monopolistic stagnation at home—monopoly being either cause or consequence of stagnation, depending on whether or not the author in question follows Keynesian reasoning on the subject—acts as a stimulus to seek fresh sources of profit abroad. But to say that monopolistic capital tries to exploit foreign countries is to say that indirectly it helps to develop them—unless one makes the totally unrealistic assumption that exploitation can be permanently divorced from development. In this fashion, American capitalism—like British capitalism in its time—does in fact bring foreign competitors into being, and it does so of necessity, as part of the process whereby capital overflows national boundaries. If this is a contradiction, it is inherent in the way the system operates, and from a Marxist standpoint there is nothing mysterious about it. The industrialization of the Third World is in fact the only major outlet still open to Western capitalism. Whether it will be undertaken depends on political variables. There is nothing in the inherent logic of the system that forbids it.

In arguing against the possibility of evolution along these lines, the more rigid adherents of the Leninist school stress the exploitative character of imperialist investment to the exclusion of all other factors, so as to arrive at the picture of a self-perpetuating pattern of neocolonialism which prevents the effective industrialization of backward countries. Magdoff is a notable practitioner of this mode of reasoning: "The integration of less developed capitalisms into the world market as reliable and continuous suppliers of their natural resources results, with rare exceptions, in a continuous dependency on the centers of monopoly control."[13] Socialist Cuba presumably is among the exceptions, though it combines heavy reliance on sugar production with total dependence on the Soviet Union and its satellites. The other Latin American countries are naturally less well placed, since they depend to a large extent on the United States, which of course makes all the difference. The reasoning affirms that integration into the world capitalist market

> has almost uniform effects on the supplying countries: 1) they depart from, or never enter, the paths of development that require independence and self-reliance; 2) they lose their economic self-sufficiency and become dependent on exports for their economic viability; 3) their industrial structure becomes adapted to the needs of supplying specialized exports at prices acceptable to the buyers, reducing thereby such flexibility of productive resources as is needed for a diversified and growing economic productivity. The familiar symptom of this process is still seen in Latin America where, despite industrialization efforts and the stimulus of two world wars, well over 90 per cent of most countries' total exports consists of the export of agricultural and mineral products.[14]

And where (it might be added) the ruling cliques or military dictatorships are free to break loose from this pattern if they choose to do so. It is true that they are not free to follow the Cuban example without provoking U.S. intervention, but they cannot be prevented from industrializing, or even from introducing state-controlled economies, as long as they do not align themselves externally with the Soviet Union or China. For the purpose of this particular argument, the emergence of national-socialist regimes all over Latin America—run by military technocrats and backed by the intelligentsia and the middle class—would be quite enough to undermine the thesis that the colonial pattern of dependence is self-perpetuating and unbreakable. It is nothing of the kind.

As a minor by-product of its dependence on Leninism-Stalinism, the Baran-Sweezy-Magdoff type of argument not only ignores Russian exploitation of Eastern Europe—supposedly liberated and presented with a socialist economy after the military take-over of 1945—it grossly inflates the importance of the cold war, a weakness shared by Kolko and other revisionist historians. This perspective makes no allowance for the basic *entente* between

Moscow and Washington, which dates back to Yalta and was kept going all through the years of political rivalry between the two blocs. The ideological frenzy of the 1950's—reinforced by Stalinist psychopathology on the one side and Dullesian drivel on the other—is taken literally by these writers, even though by now their political sympathies are engaged on the side of Cuba and China rather than the Soviet Union. The resulting picture is merely the inverted mirror image of standard U.S. cold-war literature (now going out of fashion) wherein America was seen to wage a religiously motivated struggle to save the world from the hordes of godless Communism. Standing this familiar nonsense upside down by casting the United States in the role of global aggressor results in nothing but further obfuscation. The actual competition between the two blocs led respectively by Washington and Moscow, and their highly complex relations with the various segments of the Third World, is simplified to the point of absurdity. For good measure, the burden of revolution is cast upon the peasantries of Asia, Africa, and Latin America, who are to take up where the industrial working class—now supposedly integrated into the system—left off. Thus nationalism is identified with socialism, the peasantry with the proletariat, anti-imperialism with anti-capitalism, until all the distinctions painfully elaborated in Marxist literature for a century are cast overboard in favor of a simple dichotomy: Western imperialism versus the starving masses of the Third World. People equipped with this kind of perspective no longer need a theory: practice grows out of populist sloganeering, as power is supposed to grow from gun barrels. Populism indeed is more relevant to Third World politics than Marxism. The fact is undeniable. Its consequences for the underdevelopment of socialist theorizing in the more advanced countries have yet to be faced.

For Marx, it was axiomatic that the establishment of socialism would be brought about by the industrial working class in the most advanced and civilized countries of the globe. He did not rule out the possibility of a noncapitalist form of develop-

ment in Russia, where the ancient village commune had survived
into the modern age; but he made it clear that a transition to
socialism would depend on help received from the more advanced countries of Europe, where capitalism was already fully
developed. Lenin broke with this tradition when he seized power
in 1917, on the grounds that Russia represented the "weakest
link" in the imperialist chain. He went further when in 1923
he envisaged a confrontation between "the counterrevolutionary
imperialist West and the revolutionary and nationalist East,
between the most civilized countries of the world and the Orien-
tally backward countries which, however, comprise the majority."
He did not, however, abandon the idea of a worker-peasant
alliance, which had always been central to his thinking. Russia
was to be the link between the Asian peasant and the European
or American worker.

In the Maoist perspective, the notion of such an alliance has
been abandoned. In its place there is the vision of Asia, Africa,
and Latin America, under Chinese leadership, constituting "the
storm center of the world revolution." This formulation originally arose from a factional dispute between the Russian and
Chinese leaderships, but has now acquired the force of dogma,
since it has been integrated with Chinese nationalism and
China's claim to world leadership. Its unintended consequences
include a growing convergence of U.S. and Soviet policies and
an abandonment of cold-war postures which had become habitual
while Washington and Moscow were on a collision course in
Central Europe and elsewhere. One of the odder side effects of
this realignment is the growing irrelevance of solemn historical
tracts seeking to show that the United States rather than the
Soviet Union took the initiative in unleashing the cold war in
1947—as if it mattered who fired the first shot in a "war" (fought
by proxy) to determine the exact consequences of the 1945 Yalta
and Potsdam settlements. The Chinese may be forgiven for taking no interest in this topic. Formosa, Korea, and Vietnam are
closer to home. Nor is there any good reason why anyone save

professional diplomats should get involved in tedious disputes about the origins of the cold war.

What really matters is the Maoist perspective of reliance on the Third World, and the new estimate of the peasantry's role in the "anti-imperialist struggle." Now, it should be obvious that whatever successes may be scored by national-revolutionary movements of the Vietnamese type—movements led by "classless" Communist parties drawn from the urban intelligentsia and backed by armed peasants—they cannot defeat or overthrow either capitalism or imperialism as a world system. They cannot do so for the good and sufficient reason that *no* undeveloped country can reshape the global nexus of relationships which, taken together, constitute the modern world of industrial technology (capitalist, state-capitalist, or socialist). At most, such countries can contract out and choose their own path of development. The limitations imposed upon them in this respect are fairly evident in the case of Cuba, which has to sell its sugar in a market controlled by the Soviet Union, just as Algeria has to sell its products in a market controlled by France and the other industrial economies of Western Europe. This is not to say that these countries cannot pioneer new forms of development adapted to the role of a peasantry which has rid itself of the old landowning class. What they cannot do is provide a model for more advanced societies. Nor is it the case that such upheavals demonstrate the ability of the peasantry to act as a revolutionary class. What they show is the exact opposite: the need for urban leadership if the peasants are to attain their aims. All successful agrarian uprisings in history have been led by urban elements, and the Chinese revolution is no exception. The fact that a section of the radical intelligentsia emigrated to the countryside, after it had failed to seize power in the towns, does not make its subsequent long march to victory a "peasant revolution." All it shows is that a centralized organization with a Communist ideology can survive even in a rural milieu. Since Communist parties are classless, elitist, and quite independent of the industrial proletariat even when they are based on it, this circumstance ought to occasion no surprise. Nor is it astonishing that, being patriotic and well in tune with the national tradition, the Chinese Communist Party should have taken refuge in the populist gospel.

What Maoism affirms is the natural unity of the entire people when rallied around a truly selfless leadership imbued with the proper convictions and determined to defend the national interest against domestic and foreign enemies. This ideology, which is approximately as old as the hills, has nothing in common with Marxism, but it can be described as populist socialism for want of a better term. People who sponsor such notions may be conservatives or revolutionaries, depending on circumstances not of their making. Chinese revolutionary populism is certainly the most radical doctrine ever preached to peasants by urban intellectuals. Inasmuch as it represents a commitment to "building socialism" in a precapitalist and preindustrial environment, it is likewise in an established tradition: that of the nineteenth-century Russian *Narodniki,* minus their belief in the providential role of the Slavonic peoples, which has survived in the popular Russian understanding of Leninism. Unlike Stalinism, the Chinese version does not rely solely on terror and does not aim at the liquidation of the peasantry as a class. For the rest, it is fully integrated with Chinese nationalism and ethnocentrism. This lends it a powerful appeal and makes it acceptable to the peasantry and indeed to the people as a whole. It also constitutes a reason for not confusing this kind of revolutionary nationalism with authentic socialism.

Notes

1. For a brief discussion of this topic see Paul M. Sweezy, "Obstacles to Economic Development," in C. H. Feinstein, ed., *Socialism, Capitalism and Economic Growth: Essays Presented to Maurice Dobb* (Cambridge and New York: Cambridge University Press, 1967), pp. 191–97; also Paul A. Baran and P. M. Sweezy, *Monopoly Capital* (New York: Monthly Review Press, 1966); P. A. Baran, *The Political Economy of Growth* (New York: Monthly Review Press, 1957); H. Magdoff, *The Age of Imperialism* (New York: Monthly Review Press, 1969); Peter Worsley, *The Third World* (Chicago: University of Chicago Press, 1964). For liberal and Fabian discussions of the topic see W. Arthur Lewis, *The Theory of Economic Growth* (London: Allen & Unwin University Books, 1963; Homewood, Ill.: Irwin, 1955); Hla Myint, *The Economics of the Developing Countries* (New York: Praeger, 1965); Gunnar Myrdal, *Challenge to Affluence* (New York: Vintage Books, 1965); *Asian Drama: An Inquiry into the Poverty of Nations*, 3 vols. (London: Allen Lane The Penguin Press; New York: Pantheon, 1968); *An International Economy* (London: Routledge; New York: Harper & Row, 1956); Thomas Balogh, *The Economics of Poverty* (London: Weidenfeld & Nicolson, 1955–66; New York: Macmillan, 1967). For a Trotskyist analysis see Michael Kidron, *Western Capitalism since the War* (London: Weidenfeld & Nicolson, 1968). Earlier academic writings worth consulting include K. Mandelbaum, *The Industrialization of Backward Areas* (Oxford: Basil Blackwell, 1945), and the essay collection titled *The Progress of Underdeveloped Areas*, ed. B. F. Hoselitz (Chicago: University of Chicago Press, 1952).

2. See, for example, W. W. Rostow, *The Stages of Economic Growth* (Cambridge and New York: Cambridge University Press, 1960); for a Fabian contribution to post-imperial British writing see John Strachey, *The End of Empire* (London: Gollancz, 1959; New York: Praeger, 1964).

3. Karl Marx, *Capital*, vol. 3 (Moscow, 1959), p. 245.

4. "Future Results of British Rule in India," first published in the *New York Daily Tribune*, 8 August 1853; see S. Avineri, ed., *Karl Marx on Colonialism and Modernization* (Garden City: Doubleday, 1968), p. 125. In the same article, the introduction of private property in land is described as "the great desideratum of Asiatic society."

5. *Ibid.*, pp. 128–30.

6. *Ibid.*, p. 131.

7. A. M. McBriar, *Fabian Socialism and English Politics 1884–1918* (Cambridge: Cambridge University Press, 1966; New York: Cambridge University Press, 1962), pp. 119 ff.; Bernard Semmel, *Imperialism and Social Reform:*

English Social-Imperialist Thought 1895–1914 (London: Allen & Unwin; New York: Hillary House, 1960), pp. 128 ff., 166 ff., 234 ff.

8. Michael Barratt Brown, *After Imperialism* (London: Heinemann; New York: Hillary House, 1963), p. 65.

9. *Ibid.*, p. 71.

10. *Ibid.*, p. 206.

11. For background see Tang Tsou, *America's Failure in China 1941–50*, vol. 2 (Chicago: University of Chicago Press, 1963). The author makes the interesting point (p. 478) that the China Aid Act of April 1948, which was supposed to put the moribund Chiang Kai-shek government on its feet, "brought about the most widespread and outspoken anti-American movement up to that time. This anti-American sentiment originated in the commonly held belief that Chiang was leading the country to ruin and that he · could not do so without American support." Nationalist and populist sentiments of this kind flowed into Maoist channels for reasons having very little to do with class conflict, as that term is understood by Marxists.

12. Baran, *The Political Economy of Growth*, pp. 151 ff.

13. Magdoff, *The Age of Imperialism*, p. 197.

14. *Ibid.* Magdoff also has a subsidiary line of reasoning which relies upon the financial drain imposed by foreign investment; see p. 198: Between 1950 and 1965 the flow of direct investment from the U.S. to Latin America totaled only $3.8 billion, whereas income on capital transferred to the United States came to $11.3 billion, a surplus of $7.5 billion in favor of the U.S. The corresponding figures for Europe are $8.1 billion in U.S. investment and a mere $5.5 billion in profits transferred back. The implication is that Western Europe on balance gained from American investment, whereas Latin America was a net loser. Profit rates were in fact higher in Latin America (and in the Middle East) because investments were concentrated in oil and certain minerals, and because production costs were lower than in Europe. But this merely underscores the familiar fact that "uneven development" is a source of surplus profit for the advanced countries (including the U.S.S.R.). It does not prove that no development takes place, merely that an extra price is paid for it during the critical transition period. If it be argued that development is permanently confined to a few extractive industries, then the countries in question cannot become important markets for U.S. exports.

CHAPTER 9

The Third World

AN ATTEMPT MUST NOW BE MADE TO PULL THE STRANDS of the argument together. This is not rendered easier by the fact that historical and theoretical considerations tend to get in each other's way. To take a fairly obvious instance, capitalism represents a global system which includes Japan and is therefore not coextensive with "the West," although for practical purposes the system may currently be said to have its major politico-economic center in the North Atlantic area: specifically, in the United States. Again, when one speaks of imperialism one may be tempted to look for formally constituted empires held together by military force. In this sense, the two great political alliances which have confronted each other since American and Russian troops first met on the Elbe in 1945 are "empires" controlled respectively from Washington and Moscow; but this usage, albeit hallowed by tradition, is so vague and sociologically empty as to be meaningless for analytical purposes. If there is an American Empire confronting a Soviet Empire, we may as well resign ourselves to the impossibility of saying anything concrete about imperialism in the meaning that term acquired, for liberals and socialists alike, during the first half of the present century. The ancient Chinese Empire and the imperialism described in Hobson's tract on the subject have nothing in common except the occasional employment of military force: too vague and general a criterion for any theoretical purpose.

Militarism fares no better. It is as old as history, and so is arms expenditure. As for the notion that present-day monopolistic capitalism, notably in the United States, is kept going by what is popularly known as "the arms economy," one would like to know why Japanese capitalism has managed to grow three or four times as fast as its American rival while spending only 1 per cent of the gross national product on arms. There must be something wrong with an argument that leads to such absurd conclusions. It is manifestly the case that there has been an enormous increase in unproductive public expenditure on arms—$120 billion of world spending in one year, according to a U.N. study in 1962, and a great deal more with the further escalation of conflict since that date. But the notion that this kind of waste production is burdensome only for a socialist economy, not for a capitalist one, is implausible. Individual corporations naturally profit from arms expenditure, the end product of which is stored by governments and does not compete with private firms in the market. But the resulting growth in the tax burden and in the size of the national debt interferes with normal productive investment, hinders the accumulation of capital, and renders the country in question less competitive in the world market. Taken to its logical conclusion, the arms-economy argument implies that waste production must be constantly expanded to offset stagnation and to maintain a tolerable level of employment. But in that case no significant capital accumulation would take place any longer and the system would cease to be capitalist; it would be taken over by the state and its further growth would be determined not by profits but by purely political considerations. Quite possibly something of the sort will occur one day, but capitalism will then have come to an end. Under present-day conditions, the arms economy acts as a stabilizer only insofar as it does not seriously interfere with productive investment. Hence the argument that militarism can be deduced from the logic of capitalism is invalid. An economy wholly dependent on unproductive and unprofitable public expenditure would no longer be capitalist.[1]

If it be said that the stagnation of monopolistic capitalism is just what has given rise to the phenomenon of an arms economy—the state is obliged to organize waste production because capital expansion based on profitable investment is insufficient to guarantee employment and political stability—then why is this feature so much more pronounced in the United States than elsewhere? The explanation obviously has to do with the arms race and with America's role within the world economy and the global system of political relations based upon it. But empirical considerations of this sort are extraneous to a theoretical model which deduces the necessity of an ever-growing arms budget from a long-run tendency toward stagnation. Arms production makes for inflationary price rises and is a bar to greater competitiveness, as are "limited" wars against national-revolutionary movements in Asia—quite apart from the fact that they cannot be "won" in any reasonable sense of the term. This is just why the whole issue has become a serious factor in splitting the supposedly united front of the "corporate establishment."

The only way in which the theoretical model can be linked to the arms race and the cold war is by treating entire nations—notably the United States and the Soviet Union—on the analogy of monopolistic competitors in the world market. In the present case, however, the rivals are equipped with nuclear arsenals, a circumstance that eliminates the distinction between politics and economics which was the fundamental presupposition of all previous theorizing. So far from constituting a plausible theory of imperialist competition, this kind of analogy makes it plain that the Leninist model has become unworkable. Imperialist rivalry over spheres of interest is something qualitatively different from a global confrontation in which the very existence of mankind is at stake. Such a situation was not predictable in 1920, just as the ominous possibility of a nuclear showdown between two nominally "Communist" states could not have been foreseen by Lenin and his contemporaries. To describe this state of affairs as "oligopolistic competition between whole economies" is to play with words.[2]

Insofar as the nuclear blocs compete, their aim is planetary control, not the carving out of influence spheres, an aim still pursued in the traditional manner by the lesser powers. Moreover, the East-West split, which for a while seemed to validate the Leninist schema and its Stalinist successor, is becoming increasingly irrelevant, while the North-South division between the developed countries and the rest is inexplicable on Leninist terms, since the Soviet Union—nominally a socialist country—is cast in the role of exploiter of the poor countries. NATO could still be fitted into a Leninist framework, if one were willing to accept the Stalinist picture of a world divided between "socialism" and "capitalist imperialism." The growing *détente* between Washington and Moscow and the concurrent worsening of relations between the Soviet Union and China have made the perpetuation of this kind of talk implausible. There is no reason why outsiders should oblige the surviving Stalinists by treating the cold war as the overriding political fact of the post-1945 era, when it was merely an episode in the gradual working out of a Soviet-American partnership based on tacit acceptance of a divided Europe and carefully controlled rivalry in Third World areas. A relationship of this kind does not exclude occasional hostilities, much as the informal (but highly effective) Anglo-Russian *entente* after the Napoleonic Wars did not prevent sharp conflicts over the disposal of the Turkish Empire, on one occasion (in 1853–56) even leading to war. On this analogy, the coming of the nuclear age simply means that such wars are now likely to be fought by proxy.

In practice, much of the aforesaid is recognized by New Left theorists of imperialism and anti-imperialism, which is why attention has increasingly shifted to the North-South antagonism.

Incongruous survivals of the earlier Leninist-Stalinist orthodoxy are still encountered among writers who try to make
themselves and their readers believe that U.S. foreign policy
can be analyzed in terms of capital investment. On this topic it
is best to let a professional economist speak, one who has the
additional advantage of being a socialist quite uncommitted to
the standard American attitudes on the·subject of Communist-
led revolutions abroad:

> Of our roughly $50 billion in overseas investment, some $10
> billion are in mining, oil, utility, and manufacturing facilities in
> Latin America, some 4 billion in Asia including the Near East,
> and about 2 billion in Africa. To lose these assets would deal a
> heavy blow to a number of large corporations, particularly in
> oil, and would cost the nation as a whole the loss of some $3 to
> 4 billion a year in earnings from those areas. A Marxist might
> conclude that the economic interests of a capitalist nation would
> find such a prospective loss insupportable, and that it would be
> "forced" to go to war. I do not think this is a warranted as-
> sumption, although it is undoubtedly a risk. Against a Gross Na-
> tional Product that is approaching ¾ of a trillion dollars and
> with corporate assets over 1.3 trillion, the loss of even the whole
> $16 billion in the vulnerable areas should be manageable eco-
> nomically. Whether such a takeover could be resisted politically
> —that is, whether the red flag of Communism could be success-
> fully waved by the corporate interests—is another question.[3]

It is interesting that even so well-informed and sophisticated
a writer as Heilbroner should credit the Marxist school indis-
criminately with the kind of reasoning about the decisive importance of colonial investments which Lenin inherited from
the laissez faire liberal Hobson. Contemporary Marxists are more
likely to interest themselves in the hegemonial role of U.S. capital
within the North Atlantic area than in populist fantasies about
the corporations going to war to save their assets in the Philippines.[4]

The real question is not whether the U.S. economy can survive
the loss of corporate investments in politically unstable areas—it

can and will—but what the capital flow is doing to the development of backward countries. On this issue laissez faire apologists
of "free" unregulated capitalism have traditionally had to battle
on two fronts: against socialists on the Left and nationalists on
the Right. The failure to recognize this has been among the
major weaknesses of the Marxist school. Hence in part the
Comintern's inability to understand fascism, and the bewilder-
ment of orthodox Stalinists in Cuba when faced with Castro's
victorious movement in 1959. Generally speaking, liberals and
Marxists alike have been very bad at understanding what nationalism is about. What little there is to be found in Leninist
literature on the subject of national-revolutionary movements
does not make up for this lacuna, the less so since Leninists
seem congenitally unable to admit that the decisive stratum is
not the so-called national *bourgeoisie* (which hardly exists any-
where during the preindustrial stage), but the intelligentsia. It
is the latter, at the head of the proletariat or the peasantry,
which makes up the core of all revolutionary movements in
backward countries. It is the intelligentsia which decides whether
the modernization drive shall take place under Communist,
fascist, pseudosocialist, or straightforward nationalist slogans.
And it is the intelligentsia—civilian or military, in any case
urban and classless—which seizes power. Having done so, it
establishes a dictatorship (normally in the form of the one-party
state) and imposes modernization on the masses of workers and
peasants—in the name of the people, of course. It does so through
the agency of state power. If necessary, it employs the state to
liquidate entire classes, as in Russia under Stalin. In the process,
of course, it has to turn itself into a bureaucracy, which is why
its roots in the old prerevolutionary intelligentsia tend to be
overlooked. But it is still the same elitist strategy that imposes
the "revolution from above" upon the masses, even if the old
revolutionary vanguard is exterminated by a totalitarian state
party, itself both product and prime agent of the modernization
process. The latter, needless to say, subjects workers and peasants

alike to an industrial discipline indistinguishable from that of capitalism, but it does so under conditions where the economic surplus is administered by a political bureaucracy responsible only to itself. This is where nationalism comes in, for the fusion of socialism with patriotism in the ideology of the radical intelligentsia is rendered plausible by the fact that industrial modernization appears as the precondition of national survival. A party which knows how to seize the leadership of this kind of national-revolutionary movement cannot in the long run be defeated, short of the physical destruction of the country inhabited by the population under its control.

This is not to say that such movements are bound to spring up everywhere. They may fail to emerge, in which case the society simply goes on stagnating at a preindustrial level. This fate is probably in store for a number of undeveloped countries, a circumstance which lends an edge of desperation to their politics. There is no suprahistorical law which decrees that all backward countries must witness a victorious revolution or some other break with traditional stagnation and poverty. They may fail and rot. What they cannot do is have it both ways: modernize without destroying their ancient preindustrial customs and institutions. If this destruction is not undertaken by the Communist Party, then it must be pushed through by some other agency willing and able to effect a radical break with the past. In the absence of such a rupture, the country can go on existing as a subsidiary part of some global system which one may term "imperial" if one is so minded; but it cannot raise itself to the level of the advanced industrial nations—capitalist or socialist. This is now fairly well understood. What is not always understood is the fact that in such an environment, and faced with such tasks, "Communism"—or Marxism-Leninism, to give it its official label—ceases to be the theory of anything worth being called a workers' movement. It becomes the ideology of an elitist avant-garde drawn from the intelligentsia.

The essentials of the matter are best understood if one

abstracts from special cases such as Japan's successful modernization along capitalist lines in the late nineteenth and early twentieth century. Some features of this experience are indeed of
general interest. Anyone looking for evidence that national
sovereignty is a precondition of successful all-round development
need only compare Japan's brilliant record with India's miserable
stagnation. The same applies to the usefulness of foreign investments. Japan managed very well without them, and indeed may
have owed its economic salvation to the fact that it succeeded in
keeping them out. Nonetheless it will not do to treat national
sovereignty and economic protectionism as a sufficient explanation. They were essential preconditions, no more. The opportunity still had to be grasped. Here again there is no universal
rule to be invoked. Europe, Asia, and Latin America are littered
with independent nation-states which somehow missed the boat.
There is no guarantee that modernization will produce political
stability, democracy, socialism, or anything else. There is only
the certainty that without economic development the society
will reproduce all those superstructural features which rendered
it poor and backward to begin with.[5] This is particularly the case
in regions where population presses on land and other national
resources. A country like India, whose population is expected to
double by the end of the century, is confronted with problems
for which liberalism has no solution. Unless the peasant masses
can be dragged out of their lethargy by a social revolution which
breaks the stagnation of village life and frees them from their
ancient superstitions, the prospect is one of increasing misery.

India's economic problems cannot be sensibly discussed in
abstraction from the wider issues of social conservatism, rural
backwardness and ignorance, official incompetence, and political
weakness at the center. But even in the narrowest economic
terms it is evident that present policies have failed to break the
vicious circle of poverty-stagnation-population growth-increasing
misery which has turned cities like Calcutta into cesspools and
which threatens to promote a gigantic catastrophe before the

end of the century. In this context, "foreign aid" is a relatively minor topic—certainly when compared to the ruling elite's failure since independence in 1947 to destroy the caste system, kill the cows, and get the exploding birth-rate under control. Quite clearly, such things can be done only by a dictatorship, and even a Communist dictatorship may shrink from the task, in which case the Malthusian "solution" is likely to take the form of man-made famines on an enormous scale.

Stalin broke the Russian peasantry. The Indian peasantry is going to be harder to break and there is no Indian Stalin in sight. Nor would such an apparition necessarily be welcome even to Communists, most of whom would probably be liquidated by the *apparat* along with the peasants and their cows. It is only when one considers the liberal-democratic or populist and pseudosocialist, alternatives that the need for an "iron surgeon" begins to suggest itself. Populism—in practice meaning cottage industries and agricultural development, instead of lopsided emphasis on industry—could probably be made to work if it were not for the caste system and the population explosion. Laissez faire liberalism under Indian conditions is merely a bad joke: in practice, it resolves itself into waste production and the importation of useless luxury goods for a parasitic "middle class" of bureaucrats and nonentrepreneurs. Industrialization—even if its aim could be pushed through by a renovated state bureaucracy purged of parasites—would do little to raise the productivity of farm labor, which is the precondition of everything else. As for foreign aid, its net effect has been negligible, even though in the two decades after 1947 India received, in cash or in kind, the equivalent of $11 billion.[6] All of which confirms the gloomy analysis offered by professional economists like Myrdal and Heilbroner: without a politically directed breakthrough in the decisive sector—that of agriculture—industrialization will get stuck. Nor can the breakthrough limit itself to tinkering with new crops. Unless the village population as a whole is dragged out of its customary way of life, increased productivity will only benefit a small minority of the better-off peasants at the expense of the remainder. Writing in the *New York Review of Books* on April 23, 1970, Heilbroner had this to say on the subject, in a review-article suitably headlined "Ecological Armageddon":

> The other element in the race is our ability to match population growth with food supplies, at least for a generation or so, while birth control techniques and campaigns are being perfected. Here the problem is also partly technological, partly social. The technological part involves the so-called "Green Revolution"—the development of seeds that are capable, at their best, of improving yields per acre by a factor of 300 percent, sometimes even more. The problem, however, is that these new seeds generally require irrigation and fertilizer to bring their benefits. If India alone were to apply fertilizer at the per capita level of the Netherlands, she would consume half the world's total output of fertilizer. This would require a hundredfold expansion of India's present level of fertilizer use. . . .
>
> But putting those difficulties to the side, we must recognize as well the social obstacles that a successful Green Revolution must overcome. The new seeds can only be afforded by the upper level of the peasantry—not merely because of their cost (and the cost of the required fertilizer), but because only a rich peasant can take the risk of having the crop turn out badly without himself suffering starvation. Hence the Green Revolution is likely to increase the strains of social stratification within the underdeveloped areas.

What the proponents of such solutions are after is in fact the creation of a comparatively wealthy stratum of farmers able to make use of modern methods of production. This was broadly what Stolypin tried to do in Russia after 1907, and it has been argued by some historians that he might have saved Russian capitalism (if not the Romanov dynasty) had not the 1914–18 war given Lenin his chance. Be that as it may, Russia then was—and in some respects still is—an underpopulated country, not one suffering from population pressure on the available space. The case of India is very different, and the same applies to Southeast Asia. The "Green Revolution" may do something for the agricultural output of these areas, but only at the cost of increasing social tensions. The village proletariat cannot profit from it, and the Malthusian specter is likely to raise its head at the very moment when the experts have at last managed to "solve" the problem of turning capitalist farming into a paying proposition. The disruption of the ancient subsistence economy and its replacement by a market-oriented network of commercial transactions benefit only those who already possess enough initial capital to climb onto the ladder of "rising expectations" that liberal writers of the Galbraithian school never stop celebrating. Meanwhile the rural proletariat is driven to the towns, where it forms huge agglomerations of stagnant misery. Insofar as Western "aid" speeds this process, it is counterproductive, for the effect is to promote a total rejection of the entire system. This is now happening over large areas of Asia and Latin America, and it is beginning to happen in Africa. Hence the identification of capitalism with imperialism still makes sense to intellectuals who wish to save the village community or, alternatively, to use its disintegration for the purpose of unleashing a revolutionary movement against domestic and foreign exploiters.[7]

Some of the probable consequences of this process were perceived by the Communist International as early as the 1920's, when the Russian Revolution was deliberately projected as an alternative model of development. What ruined the parties directed by the Comintern was their obstinate attachment to the Leninist-Stalinist dogma that the revolutionary movement must take place under the leadership of the industrial working class— or at least of a party based upon that class (though in practice independent of it by virtue of its centralized structure). It was only when the local Communists, or some of them, got rid of this ludicrous *idée fixe* that they were able to make headway. By now, the realization that only the intelligentsia can undertake a radical reorganization of society in backward countries is widely enough accepted for Communist parties to have become effective competitors of their fascist rivals who otherwise would have the field to themselves—as they did in Italy and Germany during the 1920's and 1930's, when the Communists heroically stuck to their archaic faith in the proletariat and were wiped out in consequence. In this context, it is important to note that leadership of Communist parties by intellectuals is not the main issue. Such leaderships existed even when the parties in question held slavishly to their belief in the "leading role" of the working class. The real break came when the intelligentsia as a group acquired an awareness of its own role and ceased to apologize for its existence. Once this had occurred, Communism could, in backward countries, become the faith of the only stratum capable of giving political leadership to the masses in town and country. The "vanguard" concept helped to still uneasy consciences, since it was explained that the party acted as the spearhead of the mass movement, as indeed it did. The only trouble was that the extreme Right could likewise throw up a vanguard of classless intellectuals, committed to radical nationalism rather than Marxism-Leninism. Then the only remaining question was which party stood a better chance of getting the national-revolutionary movement under way.

The probability, under present-day conditions, of such an internal fissure *crack* arises from the nature of the anti-imperialist movement itself. Since in a backward country all classes of the population, with the exception of a thin oligarchic stratum and a few merchants, feel cheated and exploited by foreigners, it is fatally easy to work up a head of steam behind *any* nationalist movement that promises to end this state of affairs. Such movements may be, and quite often are, national-socialist rather than Communist in orientation. Moreover, Communism is now itself split as between Moscow-oriented parties which cling to the Leninist idea of a worker-peasant alliance, Maoist groups which aim at the landless peasantry, Castroite preachers of guerrilla warfare, and Trotskyist believers in the industrial proletariat. The last-named can draw some encouragement from Syndicalist traditions in Western Europe and Latin America, but are unimportant elsewhere. All concerned operate with a questionable distinction between oligarchic allies of imperialism and a "national *bourgeoisie*" supposedly committed to industrialization and political independence. The distinction looks more satisfying on paper than in reality, where the "national *bourgeoisie*" commonly turns out to be either nonexistent or to consist of a handful of ideologues, in or out of uniform. The latter can with the greatest of ease be induced to style themselves socialists, much to the alarm of American investors unfamiliar with Saint-Simonism and unaware that "socialism" has become the universal faith of virtually all thinking people in backward countries. The only constant element in this flux is the appeal made to the intelligentsia by all the competing groups. In a sense this is also true of the situation in Western society, with the important difference that the central issue is not "development" but full employment. Moreover, an alliance between a mature industrial working class and the new technical intelligentsia, plus other white-collar groups, is something quite different from the typical populist symbiosis of an unemployed urban intelligentsia and an impoverished peasantry. It is only the latter combination that gives rise to the phenomenon of anti-imperialism in general and Maoism in particular, for it is only in poor and undeveloped countries that "socialism" can come to stand for resistance to foreign oppression and exploitation.

One may legitimately dispute the argument that it is *only* monopolistic capitalism which holds back the all-round development of the Third World.[8] That it does so is undeniable, though there are other factors as well on which Leninists prefer not to dwell—peasant conservatism for instance, and the problem of accumulating capital within the agricultural sector for investment in industry. Stagnation was after all the normal condition of most cultures until the Industrial Revolution made its appearance. The real question is not whether capitalism exploits the undeveloped countries—of course it does, and always has—but why it has not done more to revolutionize them through the very mechanism of exploitation. We have already seen that Marx overrated the impact of British industry on India at the very peak of the free-trade era, long before monopolism made its appearance. Even then capital typically flowed to lands of European settlement—North America above all—while colonial investment went largely into a few extractive industries. The technological "spin-off" from such investments, plus railway building (Lenin's favorite yardstick) was insufficient to generate anything like a genuine breakthrough, if one excepts the case of Japan where there was no direct foreign investment, albeit plenty of indirect external pressure. The pattern has not really changed in recent decades. Western society never did export the industrial revolution to genuinely backward areas, as distinct from lands of European settlement. The old stagnant cultures were not revolutionized. If they did not pull themselves up by their own bootstraps in the Japanese fashion, they went on stagnating whether they were nominally independent or not.

Nor is there any good reason to believe that the Soviet model—which, for practical purposes, means the Stalinist model—can be successfully exported to the Third World. It is true that the Russian Communist Party had to struggle with precapitalist social relations, and to that extent acquired an understanding of certain problems which the Soviet Union shared with Asia. But Russia was already launched much further along the path of industrial development than any of the authentically poor countries in today's undeveloped world, and the Russian autocracy supplied a ready-made instrument for Stalin's "revolution from above": the massive machinery of a state power which survived the Revolution practically unchanged and possessed long experience of dealing with rebellious workers and peasants. This bureaucracy could and did liquidate the peasant smallholder once it had been given orders to do so. It is unlikely that any other state machine could have smashed the peasantry as thoroughly as the Stalinist terror machine did in the 1930's, herding the bulk into collectives and shipping all recalcitrant elements off to labor camps. It is even more unlikely that the Stalinist experience will be repeated in the genuinely poor countries, whatever the degree of modernization imposed upon the masses by the political bureaucracy and the intelligentsia.

What may reasonably be expected is a growth of Maoist tendencies linked to an anti-imperialist ideology which identifies imperialism both with the West and with the Soviet Union. The likelihood of this happening arises from the mounting disparity between growth rates and expectations along the North-South axis which has begun to replace the East-West pattern of the cold war. The ideological counterpart of this split, as noted before, is the growth of populism. This may take a variety of forms—there is a fascist version of populism, which for a time was remarkably effective in Southern Europe and Latin America alike—but on the whole it seems probable that most national-revolutionary movements in the Third World will adopt Maoist variants of the faith. The Leninist version is better adapted to the needs of urban workers and intellectuals, both groups having already crossed the threshold of industrialization. For the same reason it is handicapped in competition with movements which openly bank upon the peasantry.

As noted before, all forms of populism hold in common the belief that the ethnic community is essentially classless, or would be so were it not for domestic or foreign interference. Inasmuch as the impact of capitalism produces strains within an agrarian economy centered upon the small farmer, capitalism appears as the enemy of ethnic or tribal solidarity. This is the rationale of "African socialism" and similarly structured movements in the Third World. While clearly unscientific, such beliefs express a felt loyalty to the ethnic community which may be labeled "nationalism" or "socialism," whichever term one prefers. The point is that populists experience their faith as an adherence to ancestral values *and* as a protest against the disintegration typically entailed by the capitalist form of modernization. In consequence, nationalism tends to be identified with socialism, anti-capitalism with anti-imperialism. This confusion comes about quite spontaneously as a response to the dislocation of the primitive community. Since the West is generally seen as the prime agent of such disintegration, populism normally assumes an anti-Western slant; and since it can plausibly be held that Western capital holds back the all-round development of backward countries in the interest of corporate monopolies, the anti-imperialist line of reasoning can likewise be adopted by groups or parties which are in effect committed to radical modernization and the destruction of the ancient ethnic solidarity of the community or the clan. Populist socialism kills two birds with one stone. It casts itself in the role of defender of the ancient classless community before the coming of capitalism, and it also blames imperialist monopoly capital for holding up the process of development which—if it were to take place—would explode the myth of classlessness. Hence it is a waste of time arguing with populists. They are typically able to hold contradictory beliefs with complete sincerity, and since in their terminology "the people" equals "the proletariat," no one is ever going to argue them out of their conviction that nationalism and socialism are identical.[9]

The combination of agrarian populism and radical nationalism makes up the sum and substance of the faith generally known as Maoism. From being in its origins connected with the Leninist version of Marxism, it has developed into a creed adapted to the reality of precapitalist societies which have never known genuine class conflict and are currently exposed to the impact of industrialization in its Western (capitalist) or Eastern (state-socialist) form. These societies are overwhelmingly poor and equally overwhelmingly agrarian. In their majority they are separated from the West, and from the Soviet Union, by racial as well as by socio-economic cleavages and antagonisms. Since they are not riven by class antagonism in the form familiar to all advanced industrial countries, they experience the stresses of industrialization as a challenge to the whole community assembled around the infallible party or the infallible leader. The resulting political system corresponds to the expectations of some nineteenth-century Russian *Narodniki* rather than to anything anticipated by the Marxists. It is perfectly viable until it is disintegrated by the very modernization process which the ruling party sets in motion. Liberalism and Marxism are equally beyond the horizon of people living within a structure of this kind. For the same reason, nothing that the United States or the Soviet Union says or does is likely to have the smallest impact upon the minds of radicals committed to the belief that the self-emancipation of the peasantry will automatically bring socialism in its train.

In the ideology of Maoism, China figures as a "proletarian nation" menaced by Western imperialism and Soviet "social imperialism" alike. The idea of the "proletarian nation" was originally worked out by the Italian fascists (and by some of their Syndicalist predecessors before 1914) to account for Italy's poverty. It was abandoned when fascism had failed and Italy had ceased to be poor. Conceivably, a time will come when China feels able to get on without Maoism, but the industrialization of so vast and poverty-stricken a country is not comparable to the stresses undergone by any European nation, nor was nuclear war then a possibility on the horizon. The scale on which events have shaped themselves has dwarfed the dimensions of what in Leninist parlance still figures as the age of imperialism. It is not only the capitalist nexus that threatens to involve mankind in global war. The transformation of Asia, by whatever means undertaken, must alter the world balance of power, and history tells us that changes of this magnitude are rarely accomplished peacefully.

Notes

1. Arms expenditure as an economic stabilizer is invoked by Michael Kidron, *Western Capitalism since the War* (London: Weidenfeld & Nicolson, 1968), pp. 38 ff. There are of course empirical grounds for stating that this kind of waste production is less bothersome from the standpoint of business corporations than public outlay on products (e.g., houses) that appear in the market and compete with private industry. But arms still have to be paid for out of taxes, and unproductive expenditure undertaken for political purposes —social stability, or defense against presumed foreign enemies—reduces the profitability of normal investments in the private sector. In a wholly state-controlled economy such as that of the U.S.S.R., the basic irrationality of arms expenditure—or space exploration, for that matter—translates itself immediately into a lower growth rate. Under capitalism the same result is achieved in a roundabout way, through inflation and the growth of the national debt.

2. *Ibid.*, p. 25.

3. Robert Heilbroner, "Counter-revolutionary America," in *A Dissenter's Guide to Foreign Policy*, ed. Irving Howe (New York: Praeger, 1968), pp. 254–55. The same author notes that "the total consumption of energy of all kinds (in terms of coal equivalent) for Afghanistan, Bolivia, Brazil, Burma, Ceylon, Colombia, Costa Rica, Dominican Republic, Ecuador, El Salvador, Ethiopia, Guatemala, Haiti, Honduras, India, Indonesia, Iran, Iraq, Korea, Lebanon, Nicaragua, Pakistan, Paraguay, Peru, Philippines, the U.A.R., Uruguay, and Venezuela is less than that annually consumed by West Germany alone." (p. 254).

4. See Michael Barratt Brown, *After Imperialism* (London: Heinemann; New York: Hillary House, 1963), p. 369: "Canada has become the one land to be industrialized with United States capital, but with the result that at least a third of Canada's industry is now owned by United States companies."

5. Gunnar Myrdal, "Economic Development in the Backward Countries," in Howe, *A Dissenter's Guide*, pp. 195 ff.

6. Herbert Feldman, "Aid as Imperialism?," *International Affairs*, vol. 43, no. 2 (London: Chatham House, April, 1967; Birmingham, Ala.: Banner Press, 1967). What is true of India applies in most respects also to Pakistan, where in 1966 the Federation of Chambers of Commerce and Industry complained that the country's industry was "heavily dependent on imports," and that foreign "aid" was mostly designed to provide a lucrative market for the donor countries. The problem is common to all developing countries, dependent and independent alike. This is just why it still makes sense to

speak of "imperialism"—provided one does not restrict the use of the term to one side in the cold war.

7. The pacifist variant supplies the rationale of Indian populist socialism. See Asoka Mehta, "Can India industrialize democratically?," *Dissent* (New York, spring and summer issues, 1955), reprinted in *Voices of Dissent* (New York: Grove Press, 1958), pp. 253 ff: "In the peasant sector of the economy, land distribution, village-oriented economy and voluntary labor for rural public works would provide opportunities for full employment. In handicrafts, better tools, adequate raw materials, cooperatives for credit and marketing, and protection against developed industries would provide increased and secure employment." All very well if it were not for the time factor, the swelling numbers of rural unemployed, and the impossibility of effecting land distribution on a really impressive scale under a political system which privileges the landlord and the money-lender. For the political consequences see M. Watnick, "The Appeal of Communism to the Underdeveloped Peoples," in *The Progress of Underdeveloped Areas,* ed. B. F. Hoselitz (Chicago: University of Chicago Press, 1952).

8. For a brief exposition of this thesis see Oskar Lange, *Economic Development, Planning, and International Cooperation* (New York: Monthly Review Press, 1963).

9. Nigel Harris, *Beliefs in Society* (London: C. A. Watts; New York: International Publications Service, 1968), pp. 186 ff.

Index